PRACTICAL REMOTE CONTROL PROJECTS

by

Owen Bishop

BERNARD BABANI (publishing) LTD
THE GRAMPIANS
SHEPHERDS BUSH ROAD
LONDON W6 7NF
ENGLAND

Please Note

Although every care has been taken with the production of this book to ensure that any projects, designs, modifications and/or programs, etc., contained herewith, operate in a correct and safe manner and also that any components specified are normally available in Great Britain, the Publishers do not accept responsibility in any way for the failure, including fault in design, of any project, design, modification or program to work correctly or to cause damage to any other equipment that it may be connected to or used in conjunction with, or in respect of any other damage or injury that may be so caused, nor do the Publishers accept responsibility in any way for the failure to obtain specified components.

Notice is also given that if equipment that is still under warranty is modified in any way or used or connected with home-built equipment then that warranty may be void.

First Published – July 1997

British Library Cataloguing in Publication Data

A catalogue record for this book is available from the British Library

ISBN 0 85934 413 4

Cover designed by Gregor Arthur

Printed and bound in Great Britain by Cox & Wyman Ltd, Reading

Contents

Introduction

This is a guidebook for the electronics enthusiast who has a project in mind that would benefit from remote control. Although the book contains a number of stand-alone projects for the reader to build, the scope of remote control is far wider than the list of projects would indicate. A circuit that is suitable for steering a model automobile is likely to be equally suitable for steering a model tank or a flying model aeroplane, or for steering a microwave antenna rig. The reader will readily find ways to adapt the circuits to all manner of applications. This is a book of solutions looking for problems to solve!

This book follows two books on the same subject that have been consistently popular for nearly two decades. The first, Remote Control Projects (BP73), was published in 1980, and the second, the Remote Control Handbook (BP240), was published in 1988 with a revised edition in 1994. Over the years there have been few developments in the principles of remote control (although we have managed to think up a few new techniques from time to time!), but there have been a number of advances in the technology available to implement remote control systems. BP73 relied heavily on current-hungry 7400 logic ics, which are now totally replaced by low-current technology such as CMOS and the 74HC00 series. The result is that circuits that previously required a mains power supply (or the constant replacement of heavy-duty batteries) can now be run on button-cells or similar cells with a consequent reduction in the volume and weight of equipment and an increase in portability.

A major development since 1980 is the increasing computing power available to the home constructor. In BP73 we introduced the vintage Sinclair MK-14 microprocessor system, with its 256 bytes of RAM. In BP240 we upgraded to home computers such as the Spectrum and the BBC Microcomputer. In this book we have the full power of the IBM personal computer (or its look-alikes) at our disposal, with far more megabytes of storage than we are ever likely to require in a remote control application. In more recent years attention has been turned to microcontrollers. As an example of the use of this kind of device, we describe how to program the BASIC

Stamp microcontroller. The extent of its memory is perfectly adequate for most remote control purposes and its small size, low cost, and easy programming make it preferable in many ways to a fully-fledged microcomputer.

In addition to the developments outlined above, an ever-widening range of specialised remote control ics has become available. This is both good news and bad news. As improved versions of ics are released, the older versions are gradually discontinued. When a designer specifies a particular ic in a circuit, there is no guarantee that it will be obtainable even as little as a year later. This is a fact that has to be faced by the professional designer, the manufacturer of ic-based equipment – and the hobbyist. For this reason we have implemented as many as possible of the circuit in this book with standard logic gates, flip-flops and other simple logic devices. But it is a pity not to make use of some of the cleverer ics provided by the manufacturers, so we have chosen a few of them as the basis for some of the circuits. We hope we have chosen ones which will last for as long as this book is in print. It is all a matter of guesswork. The SL490 PPM coder was featured in BP37 and is still available (at least, at the time of writing!), while its companion the 922 PPM decoder was discontinued some years ago, along with several other useful ics. We hope that you will be able to obtain every ic specified in this book but if the manufacturer or your supplier tells you that a certain ic is discontinued, try another supplier. Several years after manufacture of the 922 ceased it was still available from the stocks of individual suppliers. Shop around!

A remote control circuit, whether it is a simple one used for switching a porch-light on and off, or a complex one that controls an elaborate model-railway layout, is essentially a system. It has recognisable sections or modules with specific functions. Therefore it may be designed and assembled in a modular way. We have followed the modular approach in this book and tried to ensure that as many as possible of the modules are compatible with each other. Thus your projects can be tailor-made to suit a wide range of remote-control applications.

Owen Bishop

The Plan of this Book

Chapter 1 outlines the principles of remote control.

Chapter 2 describes the four main control channels, their suitability for different purposes, and practical details of projects for using each of these channels for simple on-off control. If you are a beginner, try one or more of these projects before going on to the later chapters.

Chapter 3 gives circuits for generating signals for more complicated control regimes, including speed control.

Chapter 4 deals with more refined control strategies, including the use of computers and microcontrollers.

Chapter 5 has detailed instructions for handling mechanical drivers, such as solenoids, servo-motors and stepper motors.

If you always use batteries to power your projects, the paragraphs below are not for you. BUT, if you ever build a project powered from the mains, read and observe these precautions.

AC Mains Precautions

If a circuit is connected to the AC mains supply, certain precautions should be taken during the construction, testing and use of the circuit:

1 If you have not previously built a mains-powered project, it is advised that you should first build one or two mains-powered projects from kits which have ready-made, professionally laid-out printed circuit boards, and include components rated to withstand the expected voltages and currents.

2 If this is your first home-designed mains-powered project, build it under the guidance of someone who is already experienced with mains-powered circuits.

3 Provide a metal or strong plastic enclosure for the project. Obtain the enclosure from a recognised supplier of electronics

components. Do not use plastic 'sandwich boxes' or other non-electronics boxes; they may easily shatter or may be a fire risk.

4 Take special care with the layout of the circuit board and the mounting of off-board components. Try to confine all components and tracks which carry mains current to one area of the board. Make all mains-carrying tracks as short as possible, and use mains-rated insulated wire to carry mains current between terminals on different parts of the board.

5 If the enclosure is made of metal, or has a metal panel, connect the earth line of the mains supply to the enclosure or panel.

6 Secure the mains cable to the inside of the enclosure, close to the point where it enters the enclosure.

7 Construction should be as robust as possible; bear in mind that at some stage the project may be dropped or suffer mechanical damage. It must be able to withstand rough handling.

8 Check that no bare metal parts or tracks that are carrying mains current can come into contact with bare metal parts that are intended to be at low voltage. Check that this can not happen if the project is dropped or distorted. It sometimes happens that a project looks safe in this respect when first mounted in the enclosure, but screwing down the lid brings bare metal parts into contact with each other, especially if a mass of bunched-up connecting wires forces the circuit board out of alignment.

9 Before plugging the circuit into the mains, use a magnifier to check the circuit board for streaks or blobs of solder that may be short-circuiting adjacent tracks. On a stripboard, use a magnifier to check that strips which should have been cut across have actually been completely cut. Look to see that there is no thin 'wire' of copper remaining around the rim of the hole, and that there are no flakes of copper still attached which might

short-circuit to adjacent tracks. Use a continuity checker to confirm that all points on the circuit that should be connected are in fact connected. Also confirm that there are no short-circuits between the mains lines, and between the mains lines and the low-voltage lines of the circuit.

10 If there are any sections of the circuit that can be tested without connecting the circuit to the mains, test these sections first.

11 Before plugging the circuit into the mains make a final check on it, comparing it point by point with the circuit diagram. Bolt the lid of the enclosure fully into place.

12 When all is correct to the best of your knowledge, test the circuit with mains power switched on. If any faults become apparent, switch off the mains supply immediately. Do not open the enclosure until you have switched off the mains supply and removed the mains plug from the socket.

13 If you have re-opened the enclosure to investigate faults, replace the lid and bolt it in place before reconnecting the circuit to the mains.

14 As an ADDITIONAL precaution (*not a substitute* for those listed above) when testing the circuit, take the mains supply from a socket equipped with a residual current device (RCD).

Chapter 1

REMOTE CONTROL SYSTEMS

To many people, the word remote describes something that is a long way away, for example, a remote highland glen. In a remote control system the remotely controlled device may be only on the other side of the room, as when we use the controller of the TV set. The fundamental principle of remote control is that the operator has no physical connection with the controlled device. We may employ remote control for convenience; the TV can be controlled from any part of the room – often from the most comfortable arm-chair. Or it may be employed to allow several devices all to be controlled from one location, as when we control the locomotives, turnouts and semaphores of a model railway from a central control panel. Or it may be for safety, as when we use remotely-controlled equipment for handling hazardous chemicals. Remote control is also used when we wish to control something that is normally inaccessible, for example, a radio relay station on a mountain-top or a soil-sampling buggy on the Moon.

Transmission

A remote control system consists essentially of a person operating a transmitter which sends signals to a receiver connected to the controlled device (Fig. 1.1). The transmission channel is usually either sound, infra-red radiation (either freely radiated or confined in an optical fibre), radio or an electrical current in a conductor. Were it not for the fact that no electronics is involved, we might say that a shepherd whistling to his dog is an example of remote control using sound. In practice, there are so many audio frequency sounds criss-crossing the air that we use only frequencies higher than the audio range (ultra-sound) in remote control. When we control a device by switching a supply of electrical power on or off (as when we switch on a ceiling lamp) we do not consider this to be remote control. Remote control by wired connection occurs when we use wires to convey pulsed or other signals (usually of low power) to the controlled device, which has an independent source of power.

1

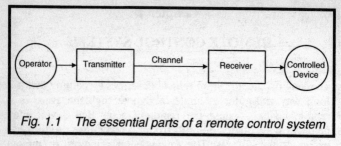

Fig. 1.1   The essential parts of a remote control system

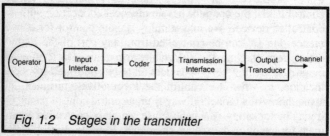

Fig. 1.2   Stages in the transmitter

Looking more closely at the transmitter (Fig. 1.2) we see that the operator makes input to the system by an input interface. Often this is a switch, push-button or key but in some systems it may be a lever (joystick) or a device such as a computer mouse. The mechanism of this drives a circuit, a coder, which produces an appropriate electrical signal. We have more to say about coded signals later. The signal is then prepared for transmission by the transmission interface. It may be amplified, perhaps filtered, and sometimes modulated on to a carrier signal. The output transducer converts the energy of the electrical signal to another form: ultra sound, infra red radiation, or electromagnetic radiation at radio-frequency. Thus the transducer is either an ultrasonic crystal, an LED, possibly a laser, or a radio antenna.

Reception
The transmitted energy is received by a sensor or transducer (Fig. 1.3) such as an ultrasonic crystal, a photodiode or phototransistor, or a radio receiving antenna. In the receiving interface the incoming energy is used to produce an electrical

2

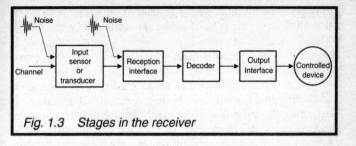

Fig. 1.3   Stages in the receiver

signal which is, as closely as possible, a replica of the original electrical signal. Because the energy received may be only a small portion of that which was transmitted, this stage usually involved amplification. It may also involve filtering, for it is during transmission that noise may be introduced into the system. Broadly speaking, noise is any sort of signal that is not intended to be present. In a sound system, noise may include sounds that we commonly call noise, such as the sound of a dropped dustbin lid. But, in a sound-based remote control system, noise comprise all manner of sounds from the bark of a dog to the tones of a symphony orchestra. Any of these, inadvertently received, can distort the control signal to the extent of rendering it unclear or totally ineffective. In an infra-red system, noise may include visible light from nearby lamps (particularly filament lamps which generate appreciable infra-red), emissions from fires or heaters, and possibly signals from other infra-red controllers. Optical fibre systems are particularly free from noise of this kind. In radio systems, there may be transmissions from local radio stations or electromagnetic interference caused by the switching of motors, automobile ignition systems, and thunderstorms. Remote control systems are designed to prevent such noise from entering the system or to eliminate its effects if it does gain entry.

Noise, mainly electromagnetic, may also enter any system in the reception interface, when electromagnetic fields cause currents to be induced in the conductors or coils of the circuit. It may be necessary to shield the circuit to prevent this. Noise may be generated in the components of the circuit itself, especially in resistors and transistors. It may also originate in earlier stages in the system, for example a faulty button switch

3

may generate multiple pulses instead of only one. With attention to design, this type of noise can normally be prevented. The elimination of noise is particularly important where the signal is weak, which is mainly in the input sensor or transducer stages, or in the early stages of amplification within the reception interface. Here the noise may rank in magnitude with the signal itself and both are amplified together. In extremes, the noise may be so great that it saturates the sensor and swamps the signal. It is less likely for noise to be introduced in significant quantities in later stages for, by then, the signal will have adequate strength. We discuss practical examples of noise prevention and elimination as they arise in the various projects.

Assuming that the signal leaving the reception interface has been suitably amplified and is satisfactorily noise-free, it then passes to a decoder. This interprets the meaning of the signal in terms of what the controlled device is required to do. The decoded signal operates on the output interface, sending power to one or more drivers (solenoids, motors, lamps) in the controlled device to produce the required action.

Feedback

In a systems such as that already described there is a one-way transit of the signal from the operator to the controlled device. This may be satisfactory when the operator can see the device responding. But there are many links in the chain of control, any of which may be broken with the result that control is lost. The situation is that of *open-loop control*, as described in our companion book *Practical Electronic Control Projects* (BP377). In many cases it is desirable to add feedback to the system, making it a *closed-loop system* (Fig. 1.4). In its simplest form a simple visual signal such as a flash of light from an LED is all that is required. This is often used on radio and TV remote control systems. An LED mounted on the front panel of the radio or TV set flashes briefly whenever a signal has been received from the controller. In other instances a short beep from a sounder fulfils the same function. If many actions of the controlled device have to be monitored, it may be necessary to incorporate coding into the feedback transmitter and decoding into the feedback receiver.

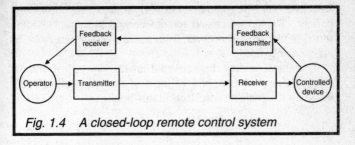

Fig. 1.4   A closed-loop remote control system

Note that there are two levels of feedback information. The first level is feedback from the receiver circuit, simply to acknowledge that the transmission has been received. In the second level there is feedback from the controlled device itself. For example, there may be a position sensor to detect when a certain part of the controlled mechanism has reached the required position. This sends a signal to that effect back to the operator. Perhaps one of the more complex examples of this type of feedback is the TV camera on a Moon buggy which records images of the operations of the buggy for transmission back to Earth.

Remote Sensing
One example of remote sensing, or measurement at a distance, is the satellite with sensors to detect radiation of various wavelengths emanating from the Earth below. This has little in common with remote control. Another example of remote sensing is when an instrument such as a seismometer or thermometer is placed in the crater of an active volcano and transmits data about seismic movements and temperature to recording devices situated well outside the danger area. This second type of remote sensing is remote control in reverse. The operator of Figure 1.1 is replaced by the remote sensor, and the controlled device is replaced by the operator, taking readings on the display of the receiver unit.

Computer Control
Computers and microcontrollers can substitute for logic circuitry in the system, particularly in coding and decoding and in the processing and interpretation of signals. They can also

substitute for the human operator, at least for prolonged periods. Totally automated remote control systems are often found in industrial processes, from nuclear power generation to car assembly lines.

This brief survey has covered many aspects of remote control. Practical examples of most of these aspects are provided by the projects described in this book.

Chapter 2

CHANNELS

The four most common ways of carrying signals from the transmitter to the receiver are:

> A Ultrasound
> B Infra-red (radiated or by optical fibre)
> C Cable
> D Radio

The first stage of planning a remote control project is to decide which of these channels is to be used. Each has its own advantages and disadvantages, depending on the application that you have in mind. Later in the chapter we show how to build simple transmitters and receivers for each of these channels.

Choosing the Channel

A Ultrasound

Ultrasound is sound of such high pitch, or frequency, that it can not be heard by the human ear. The ear normally can hear sounds up to 20kHz, but a typical ultrasound transducer operates at a frequency of 40kHz. Various animals such as dogs and many insects can hear ultrasound; this is the basis of several 'dog deterrent' devices intended to keep dogs out of your garden by producing a sound that is loud and unpleasant to dogs but which can not be heard by humans.

Ultrasound transducers are relatively inexpensive and the circuits required are simple to build and align. This makes ultrasound a good choice for the beginner. Its main disadvantage is that the range is limited to about 5m, but this is adequate for the majority of domestic and hobby applications.

The wavelength of ultrasound at 40kHz is a little less than 8mm. This is far less than the wavelengths of the frequencies present in the human voice, which average 2m. Most of the sounds we hear in everyday life have wavelengths exceeding 1m. Since the furniture and other objects in a room (including

7

people) have dimensions that are appreciably smaller than the wavelengths of everyday sounds, the sound waves are *diffracted* around them. That is to say, the waves spread out as they pass the object and meet again behind it. The object does not cast any 'sound shadow'. If somebody stands between you and a radio set, you can still hear the broadcast quite well. Similarly, if you are hiding behind a tree, you can be heard on the other side when you sneeze. Conversely, when sound passes through an opening that is narrower than its wavelength, it spreads out on the other side of the opening and appears to originate from the opening. The result is that, if you listen by a window or doorway, you can hear conversation occurring in the room without actually being able to see the speakers.

Ultrasound too is diffracted around objects and through narrow openings but, because ultrasound has such a short wavelength, the objects and openings have to be much smaller for the effect to be noticeable. Objects of the size of furniture and people and openings of the size of windows and doorways are so large in relation to the wavelength of ultrasound that diffraction has little effect. The waves do not spread around the object and meet behind it. Instead the object casts a 'sound shadow'. If a person stands between the ultrasonic transmitter and receiver, the transmission is blocked. Even a hand placed between them can prevent the transmission. It is important to remember this when using ultrasound for remote control. Even though you may be able to hear sounds being made by a controlled model, the receiver in the model may not be able to hear the ultrasound from the controller unit. If you wish to transmit ultrasound from room to room, you must have an open 'line-of-sight' between transmitter and receiver. An alternative is to place a smooth firm surface at the doorway to catch and re-direct the beam from the transmitter. The beam from an ultrasound transducer is a fairly concentrated one, spreading out by about 20°. Conversely, the receiving transducer has an angle of acceptance of about 20°. This means that the transmitter needs to be aimed reasonably accurately at the receiver and to be within its angle of acceptance.

Summing up, ultrasound is inexpensive, easily built, and ideal for the beginner. Diffraction means that care must be taken in directing the transmitter and receiver. It works just as well outdoors as indoors.

B Infra-red

This is the channel most often used. Infra-red (IR) light-emitting diodes (LEDs) are cheap and two or three of them can be wired in parallel to give increased range. Usually the transmitting range is several metres, which is adequate for most applications. The transmitter circuit can be nothing more complicated than a push-button to apply power to the LED. The receiving sensor is usually an IR photodiode, which is a photodiode with enhanced sensitivity in the IR band. Receiver circuits tend to be moderately complicated because the amount of energy arriving at the sensor is often small, making it necessary for the signal to be amplified. Moreover there is often interference (noise, see Chapter 1) from other sources of IR in the same room and also from bright sources of visible light. This must be eliminated by optical filtering, electronic filtering, and often by employing more elaborate signalling strategies (Chapter 3). Simple short-range (2m-3m) circuits are easily built by the beginner.

Infra-red control usually relies on dispersing the radiation in a broad beam, which is reflected from furniture and walls to bathe the room in IR. Thus, although it is necessary to aim the transmitter carefully to achieve maximum range, there is no need for such accuracy at shorter ranges.

Outdoors the sensor tends to be swamped by bright daylight, especially by direct sunlight. Although it is possible to use a lens to concentrate the beam and to use tubular shields to exclude extraneous light from the receiver, this is rarely worth while, because it increases the problems of lining up the transmitter and receiver. When optical fibre is used to link the transmitter with the receiver, the transmitter (usually an IR LED or laser diode) directs its beam into one end of a glass fibre. The fibre consists of a thread or core of glass about 0.1mm in diameter, on which is coated a cladding of glass or plastic. The refractive index of the cladding is higher than that of the glass core so that light is totally internally reflected whenever it strikes the boundary between core and cladding. The fibre can be curved without affecting the passage of light, which means that there is no need for a line-of sight between transmitter and receiver. Also the fibre can be threaded through small holes in panels or enclosures, without affecting the light beam. In short, the fibre can carry the light to the exact place at which it is wanted, even if this is somewhat inaccessible. The light passes along the fibre being continually reflected until it reaches the other end and is detected by an IR photodiode. The material of the core has exceptional purity so that light may pass along it for considerable distance (a hundred metres or more) without excessive absorption.

The connection at the transmitting and receiving ends of the fibre is proof against external light. Also light can not enter the fibre through the cladding around the fibre. This means that optical fibre is highly immune from noise. Thus it is ideal for data transmission and is extensively used in long-distance telephone networks and in the dissemination of TV programmes in local areas. In remote control applications its main disadvantage is that there must be the physical connection of the fibre between transmitter and receiver. Transmitter LEDs and receiver photodiodes intended for use with optical fibre are often fairly expensive but there are cheap versions available which are suitable for use at distances up to 20m. It is also possible to attach ordinary LEDs and photodiodes to the ends of a length of glass fibre; such home-made units are less efficient but usable over limited distances.

To sum up, IR is one of the best channels to use for domestic and indoor hobby applications. If you need to control a device which is relatively inaccessible, or out of direct line of sight, and possibly up to 20m away, use optical fibre. On the other hand, if you are thinking of using optical fibre, you should also consider using a cable connection.

C Cable
A wired connection, like optical fibre, provides a virtually noise-free control channel. Also, since no transducers are involved, the circuitry is simpler and there is usually no need for amplification. It is true that a cable may pick up noise in the form of electromagnetic interference but this can usually be minimised by using shielded cable, with the shield connected to earth at one end of the cable.

In most systems the cable need be only a pair of light-duty wires. This carries a low-voltage, low-current signal. The signal may be simply an on/off control. A more complicated coded signal may be used to control many functions in the controlled device yet is carried by using only one pair of wires. When controlling a system which comprises several mains-powered motors, it is safer and less expensive in cable to control these by a low-voltage cable than to have a switchboard with long mains leads running to the motors.

A variant of cable-control is to use the mains wiring existing in a building for carrying control signals. This is an economical scheme, and several manufacturers produce units designed for this purpose. One or more control modules are connected to the mains wiring and these send coded signals along to receivers situated in other rooms. When a receiver detects a signal that it recognises is designated for it, it responds appropriately, for example by switching on a heater or operating a pump. Sensor units connected to the system can be used for monitoring temperature, carbon dioxide levels and other data. An advantage of control through the mains wiring is that we have a ready-made route for distributing signals throughout the building. Moreover it is easy to make changes to the system. A transmitter or receiver can be shifted to another room simply by plugging it into a different mains outlet socket. There is no expense or disruption caused by having to re-wire the system. Kits are available for the construction of mains-transmission systems, but the construction of circuits which make direct connections to the mains is a task only for the most experienced. We recommend that the reader who wishes to install this type of system should either purchase a kit and follow the instructions very carefully, or buy commercially-built units that need only to be plugged into the mains sockets.

Summing up, cable is useful for controlling fixed devices that have several functions to be controlled. A model railway system is an example, though in this case the rails acts as the cable.

D Radio
Radio control has the advantages of operating over a far greater range than ultrasound or infra-red, and of not requiring the

physical connection essential for cable control. It is particularly popular for the control of model aircraft, vehicles and boats. There are numerous control systems available commercially and, if your main interest is with the controlled models it is better to buy a ready-made system. If you wish to design and build your own radio-control system, the difficulty is that radio transmission is the subject of stringent government control in almost all countries. It is necessary for equipment to be approved and the operator to be licensed. This puts the construction of most kinds of radio control system out of reach of all but the most expert amateur. Fortunately, the home constructor is catered for by a special dispensation which allows the use of approved equipment in the 418MHz waveband without licensing requirements. Ready-made 418MHz transmitter and receiver modules are available at moderate cost and are easy to use for sending and receiving sequences of control pulses. Some have built-in circuits for generating security codes.

An Ultrasonic System

Transmitter

The construction of this circuit and its companion receiver is described in more detail than in later projects. If you are a beginner, re-read this project before attempting a new one.

Figure 2.1 shows the circuit of a complete ultrasonic transmitter. This circuit together with the receiver illustrated in Figure 2.2 make up a system for single-pulse or 'on-off' control. That is to say, the controlled device runs when the button S1 is pressed and stops running when it is released. In Chapter 3 we shall show how to use the same transmitter and receiver for more complicated control functions. You can build this pair of circuits as your first exploration of the world of remote control and extend it later.

The transducer (sometimes referred to in the catalogues as a *transmitter*) is a crystal (Xtal1 in Fig. 2.1) specially ground to resonate vigorously when a 40kHz electrical signal is applied across its terminals. The signal is generated by the oscillator circuit comprising the NAND gates 1 and 2 with their associated resistors and capacitor. These form an astable multivibrator,

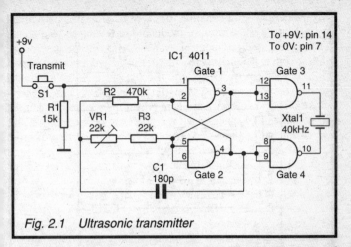

Fig. 2.1   Ultrasonic transmitter

which alternates between two states. In one state the output of gate 1 is high (+9V) and the output of gate 2 is low (0V). In the other state the output of gate 1 is low and that of gate 2 is high. The multivibrator alternates between these two states at a rate dependent on the value of the capacitor C1 and of the resistors. With the values shown, it changes state 40,000 times per second, the rate required to make the crystal resonate and produce ultrasound.

The outputs of gates 1 and 2 are fed to gates 3 and 4. Each of gates 3 and 4 gate has its inputs wired together, causing the gate to act as an INVERT gate. The purpose of these gates is to make the pulses squarer and also to act as buffers, so that there is power to drive subsequent stages without interfering with the operation of the oscillator. The gates invert the outputs from the oscillator but this makes no difference to the operation of the circuit since we still have one output low and the other output high in each cycle. The result is that, at one instant, there is a 9V potential difference across Xtal1 and half a cycle later there is 9V pd across it, but in the opposite direction. This rapid alternation of pd causes the crystal to change shape rapidly and, since the change of direction occurs at a frequency close to the natural rate at which the crystal oscillates mechanically, the crystal vibrates very strongly. It acts as a loudspeaker producing ultrasound at 40kHz.

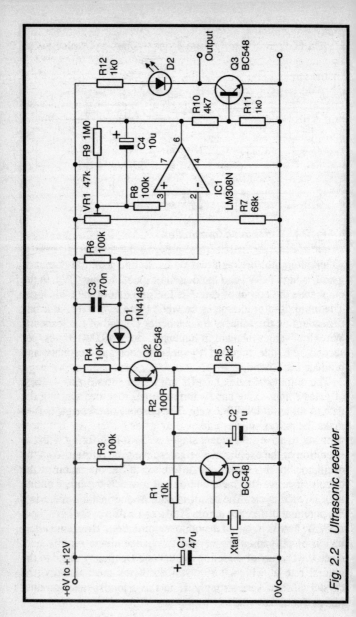

Fig. 2.2 Ultrasonic receiver

14

Static precautions

CMOS and many other ics are prone to damage by electrostatic charges and these are readily generated on the human body by movement. For example, by walking across a nylon-carpeted room you can accumulate a charge of several hundred volts on your body. The actual amount of charge is small but the potential is high and can easily 'spark' through the insulation of a CMOS gate and destroy it. Although manufacturers protect their ics by incorporating diodes to short-circuit externally-applied charges, it is best not to rely exclusively on these. Precautions include:

1) Leave the ic in its anti-static packing until you are ready to use it.
2) Carry out all construction work on an earthed metal surface, for example, a baking tray wired to the nearest cold-water pipe.
3) Do not wear clothes made from 100% synthetic fibre (eg polyester) when handling CMOS. Preferably roll up your sleeves and rest your forearm on the metal sheet when soldering.
4) Earth the bit of the soldering iron.
5) Metal tools, especially those with sharp points, may discharge to CMOS ics from a distance of several millimetres. Touch these tools against the metal sheet frequently to discharge them immediately before use.
6) Assemble the circuit except for the ics; solder in (or plug in) the ics last of all.

A number of anti-static products such as conductive mats and wrist-straps can be purchased, but these are intended for those who are working full-time in assembling or servicing electronic equipment. By observing the simple precautions listed above, the hobbyist runs little risk of static damage.

One further precaution with CMOS ics, not related to static damage, is to obey the rule:

First on, last off

This applies to applying power to the circuit when testing it during assembly. Never apply logical high levels to inputs terminals of CMOS ics without first making sure that the ic is receiving power supply to its positive power input (V_{DD}) pin and that its negative power input (V_{SS}) pin is connected to 0V (ground). Conversely, always disconnect all logical high inputs before turning off the power supply.

Construction

The four gates are conveniently provided by a 4011 CMOS ic, which contains four 2-input NAND gates. The ic has very low current consumption so the transmitter can be run for many days from a PP3 battery. The circuit is assembled on a small circuit board; design and etch your own pcb, or lay out the circuit on 2.54mm matrix stripboard. It is preferable to mount the ic in a socket (14-pin double in-line) so that the ic can be removed for testing and possible replacing if the circuit does not work. Use a battery clip to connect the battery to the circuit. Small plastic cases suitable for hand-held projects are available to complete the project; the enclosure may have a built-in battery compartment. The ultrasonic crystals are usually sold in matched pairs, one transmitter crystal and one receiver crystal, distinguished often by dots of coloured paint. Make sure that you use the correct crystal. The transmitter crystal is mounted at the front of the case, so that the beam of ultrasound is directed forward. Place the push-button so that it is in the most comfortable position for operation by the thumb.

Testing

The whole circuit should be completed (except for the crystal) and checked for correct wiring and the absence of solder bridges, dry joints and other defects before it is tested. A particularly frequent source of error may arise when ic sockets are used on stripboard. Normally the copper strips are cut beneath the socket so that pins on opposite sides of the ic are not connected together. Even when using the proper tool, a spot face cutter, it is easy to leave a microscopically thin 'wire' of copper joining two supposedly separated strips. Examine the cut using a hand lens to check that no connection remains. It can also happen that small flakes of the copper track remain attached at the cut ends and may turn to one side, so making a short-circuit with an adjacent track. Use a hand lens to look for this. It is also worth while to use a hand lens to examine all soldered joints when assembly is complete.

Before the transducer is connected into the circuit, use an oscilloscope to monitor the operation of the oscillator. If an oscilloscope is not available, slow down the operation of the circuit by temporarily connecting a 100μF capacitor in parallel with C1. This reduces the frequency to 0.1Hz (one oscillation in 10 seconds), which will give you ample time to investigate the circuit with a voltmeter. The frequency of the circuit is finally set to 40kHz by adjusting VR1, but this is best left until the receiver has been built.

Receiver

The receiver (Fig. 2.2) uses a matching crystal to detect ultrasound at 40kHz. It vibrates strongly when ultrasound of the correct frequency arrives and generates an electrical signal at this frequency. The fact that it vibrates strongly only when it received a signal of the correct frequency means that other sounds have a negligible effect and the receiver operates selectively in a noisy environment. The electrical signal is amplified by Q1 and Q2, rectified by D1, producing a fall in the voltage at the anode of D1, and hence at the (–) input of the op amp IC1. This causes the output (pin 6) of the op amp to rise. This rise is fed back through C4 and R9 to the (+) input. This is positive feedback so the op amp latches with its output high. This high output turns on Q3, producing a low output at its collector and turning on the LED indicating lamp D2. When the input pulse ceases C4 discharges through R9, the voltage at the (+) input falls and the output at pin 6 falls too. The variable resistor VR1 sets the level at which the op amp latches.

The LED is optional and may be omitted if not required.

Construction

The LM308N op amp operates on a dual supply ranging from ±2V to ±18V so the circuit can be run on a 4.5V battery, a 5V supply suited to logic ics, or on batteries of higher voltage. For greatest portability, run it on a 9V PP3 battery, as used for the transmitter. Current requirements are low since the op amp takes only 0.3mA. Current requirements are largely set by the type of LED used. Use a low-current LED for greatest economy. If power supplies are ample, a superbright LED may be preferred. It is likely that the value of R12 may need adjusting to take account of the type of LED used and the operating voltage.

Instead of or as well as an LED and resistor, a relay may be fitted in the collector circuit of Q3 (Fig. 2.3). This allows for a device such as a solenoid or motor, possibly mains-powered, to be switched by remote control. Most miniature and sub-miniature relays are suitable as they require only 10-30mA. If the relay requires a current greater than 100mA, Q3 should be replaced by a transistor of higher rating, such as a ZTX300. If neither the LED nor a relay are fitted, the circuit still requires R12 as a pull-up resistor. Other ways of driving output devices and points on choosing relays are considered later in this chapter.

With reasonably compact layout the whole circuit can be accommodated on a piece of 2.54mm matrix stripboard, about 15 strips wide and 30 holes long. This provides space for an ic to decode the output should a more complex signalling routine

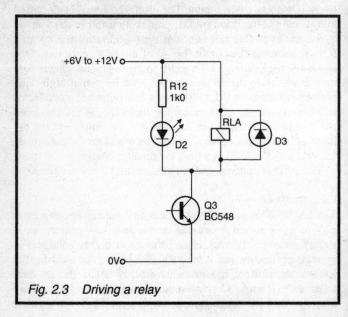

Fig. 2.3   Driving a relay

be used (see Chapter 3). There are no difficulties in assembling the circuit. As with the transmitter, it is recommended that a socket should be used for IC1. The ultrasonic receiver Xtal1 has two terminals, one of which is connected to its casing; this terminal should be connected to the ground (0V) line of the circuit. Mount the crystal where it is freely exposed to the ultrasonic signal, remembering that quite small objects can cast sound shadows and that the angle of acceptance is only about 20°. The circuit may be housed in its own case, with the crystal mounted on the outside, but space may often be found for it in the controlled device, with the crystal mounted in an exposed position. Take care that metal parts of the controlled device do not short-circuit the tracks of the circuit board or its terminal pins.

Testing

The whole circuit should be completed and checked for correct wiring and the absence of solder bridges, dry joints and other defects before it is tested. If the LED has been included, use this to check that the circuit is working properly. If not, use a voltmeter to measure the voltage at the collector of Q3, as in Figure 2.4. Then a low voltage corresponds with the LED being on in the description below. When power is first applied to the circuit, the LED may emit a brief flash, though this may not

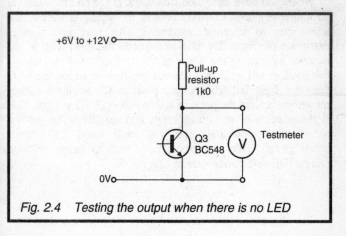

Fig. 2.4   Testing the output when there is no LED

happen at first testing. Instead, the LED may shine continuously, indicating that the wiper of VR1 is set too near to the positive rail. If this is so, turn VR1 until the LED goes off; alternatively, if you are testing as in Fig 2.4, turn VR1 until the voltmeter reads 'high'.

The action of the receiver may now be tested by using the transmitter with its crystal pointing toward the receiver crystal and about 1 metre away from it. The LED should light immediately the 'transmit' button is pressed. It should stay lit until a fraction of a second after the button has been released.

If the receiver shows no response, the fault probably lies with the transmitter; its oscillator may not be in perfect resonance with the transmitter crystal at 40kHz. Adjust VR1 of the transmitter while holding down the 'transmit' button, until the receiver shows a response by the lighting of the LED. Then gradually increase the separation of the two crystals, keeping them pointing at each other. Their action is very directional and, though the system will work well even when they are not closely lined up, maximum range can be attained only if they are directed along the same axis. A range of 4m or more should be readily attainable, but much depends upon the nature of the surfaces of walls, floors and furniture. Range is relatively great along a narrow corridor, especially if it lacks carpets and soft furnishings.

When you have exceeded maximum range and the receiver no longer responds to transmissions, try adjusting VR1 of the transmitter to improve resonance. This may give further extension of range. Try also to improve the sensitivity of the receiver by turning the wiper of VR1 (of the receiver) toward the positive rail until you reach a position in which the LED does not light but from which position the slightest further movement toward the positive rail causes the LED to light. This is the position of maximum range and sensitivity. To put the receiver to practical use you will need to add a driver circuit. This switches devices such as lamps, motors, relays. Full descriptions are in Chapter 5.

An infra-red system

Transmitter

Two versions of a simple single-pulse transmitter are shown in Figure 2.5. The TIL38 and similar IR emitters are useful in medium-power transmitters. The maximum current that these emitters can carry is 100–150mA so the resistor R1 is chosen to give a current close to that value if maximum range is to be attained. Knowing that the forward voltage drop (V_F) across the LED is around 1.5V at maximum current (the precise value depends upon the type, and is usually quoted in the catalogues), we can calculate what value of resistor is required with a given supply current:

$$R = \frac{\text{supply voltage} - \text{voltage drop}}{\text{maximum current}}$$

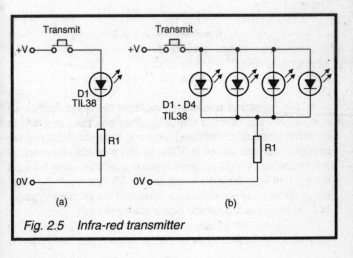

Fig. 2.5   Infra-red transmitter

For example, if the supply voltage is 6V, the voltage drop is 1.5V and the maximum current is 0.15A, the required resistor is:

$$R = \frac{6 - 1.5}{0.15} = 30\Omega$$

It may be necessary to use a resistor rated at more than the usual 0.25W or 0.125W. To calculate the resistor wattage:

$$P = \text{voltage drop} \times \text{maximum current}$$

In the example above:

$$P = 1.5 \times 0.15 = 0.225W$$

A 0.25 W resistor is adequate, though an 0.5W resistor would be preferred to prevent overheating.

A single LED without a reflector or lens to focus a beam has a range of about 1m. To increase the range, simply add more LEDs in parallel, as in Fig 2.5b. The same equations as above may be used to find the value of the resistor, multiplying the current by the number of LEDs. For example for 4 LEDs, as above:

$$R = \frac{6 - 1.5}{4 \times 0.15} = 7.5\Omega$$

and
$$P = 1.5 \times 4 \times 0.15 = 0.9W$$

A 1W resistor is needed. To increase the range further we can employ one or more GaAs (gallium arsenide) or GaAlAs (gallium aluminium arsenide) emitters. Some of these operate at higher currents (often at 500mA) and produce higher intensity radiation. A wide range of types is available, with different ratings and with different beam angles. The narrower the beam angle the more concentrated the beam and the greater the range, but one has to aim a narrow beam more precisely.

The figures quoted above apply to an emitter that is running continuously. Emitters can be run at much higher currents and thus with much greater output of IR, provided that they run for only a short period of time, with a resting time between to allow them to cool. For example, the TIL38 can be run with a current of up to 2A provided that the pulse length is limited to 10μs and pulses are produced no more often than once per millisecond. Certain high-power GaAs emitters can run at 10A, increasing their radiant power 40 times. This short intense flash of radiation has a much greater range. Or we can operate at the same range but in brighter lighting conditions. Figure 2.6 is a circuit of a transmitter operating on this principle. IC1 is the CMOS version of the popular 555 timer, here wired as an astable. The diodes D2 and D3 permit the 'on' (high output) period to be shorter than the 'off' (low output) period. When the button S1 is pressed, the power is switched on; D1 is a regular LED which comes on to indicate that the transmitter is operating. IC1 begins to oscillate. With the values given in Figure 2.6 it is on for 10μs and off for 1ms.

The output from IC1 goes to an n-channel MOSFET, Q1. There are many power MOSFETs which can be used here, a subject discussed at the beginning of Chapter 5. The two factors to take into account are the current rating, which should be at least as high as that of the infra-red LED (D4). The other factor is the 'on' resistance which should be less than 0.1Ω. Two suitable types are the BUZ10, rated at 20A, with 0.08Ω 'on' resistance, and (for the most powerful emitters) the BUZ11, rated at 30A and 0.03Ω. Several of the gallium arsenide emitters can operate on a 10μs pulse of 10A, which gives a much extended operating range.

One final point about transmitters is that the miniature IR LEDs such as the TIL32 are not suitable because of their low emission. They are intended only for close-range detection, such as in punched-card reading.

Construction
The unit is best housed in an enclosure purpose-made for a hand-held remote control. This may have a compartment and clip for the PP3 battery. Mount the LED(s) pointing forward. Mount the push-button on the top surface of the case, conveniently placed for thumb operation. The value of R4 depends on the current rating of the LED. With some high-current LEDs

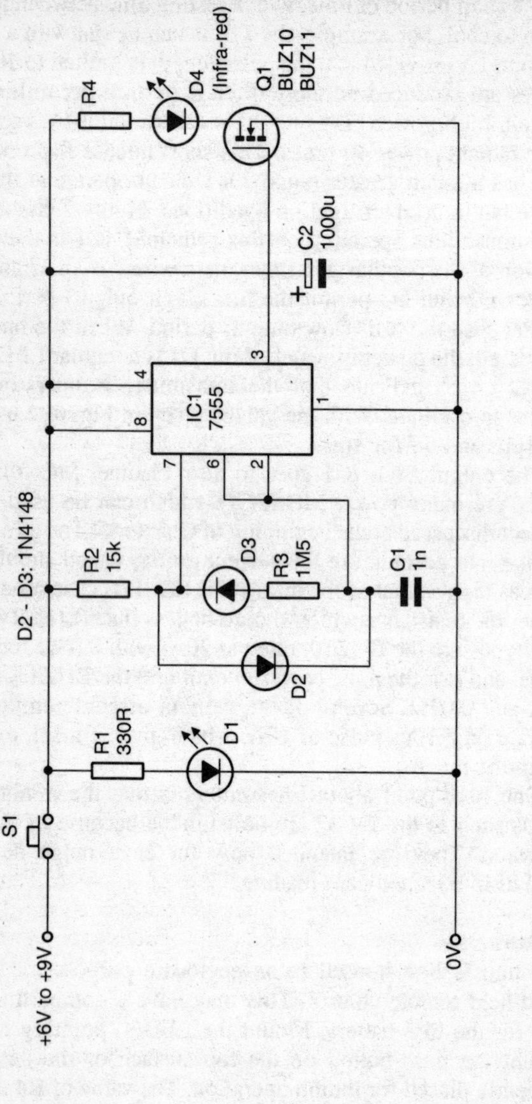

Fig. 2.6 Circuit for high-intensity flashing

R4 may be omitted; see below for a technique for discovering a suitable value.

Testing
Assemble the whole circuit before testing, using a 15kΩ resistor for R4 to restrict the current to a level suitable for continuous running. Temporarily wire a 10μF capacitor in parallel with C1 to increase timing periods to 0.1s on and 10s off. Use a voltmeter to monitor the output of IC1 at pin 3, and also the voltage at the drain of Q1. Voltage should fall almost to 0V for 0.1s every 10s. A guide to the correct value of R4 is obtained by measuring the forward voltage across D4. During the 'off' period this is zero but rises during the 'on' period. You may prefer to wire a 1000μF capacitor in parallel with C1 to increase the 'on' period to 10s to allow time for measuring the voltage. The voltage should be no more than the forward voltage specified in the catalogues. This is usually about 1.7V for a current of 100mA. With high-power GaAs emitters running at the current of several amps the only way is to use an oscilloscope to measure the peak forward voltage without any other capacitor in parallel with C1. The most powerful GaAs emitter when pulsed at 10A have a forward voltage of 4V or more. It is safer to start with R4 greater than expected, and gradually reduce it while taking readings, until the allowable forward voltage is attained. You may be able to omit R4 altogether, replacing it with a wire link.

Receiver
A simple IR receiver is shown in Figure 2.7. It uses an IR photodiode as its sensor. The case of this is relatively opaque to visible light (it appears black) but is transparent to IR. Unfortunately, sunlight and light from filament lamps and high-intensity fluorescent lamps contains a strong IR component. Outdoors or in a brightly-lit room this may saturate the photodiode and prevent the receiver from working. There are several ways to minimise this:

1) Screen the photodiode from external sources as far as possible. This is a simple precaution but limits the angle of acceptable of the receiver.

25

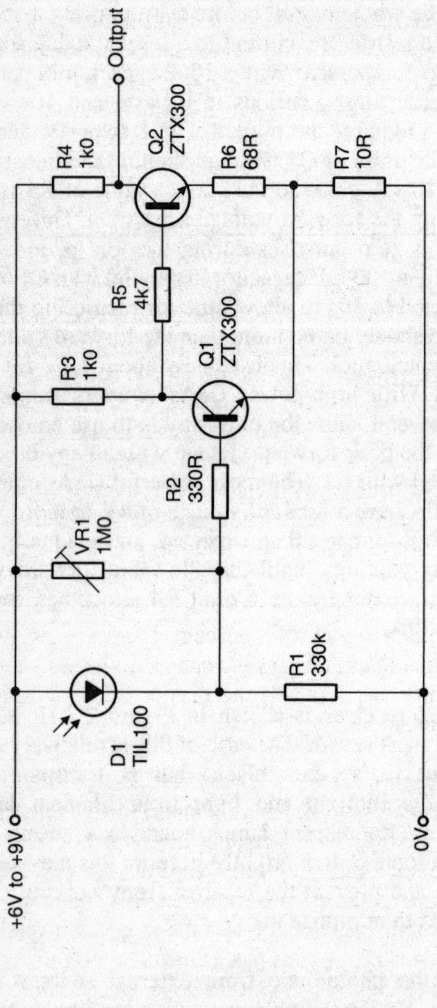

Fig. 2.7 Infra-red receiver

2) Use a strong IR source in the transmitter, either 3 or more LEDs or a high-current pulse circuit such as Figure 2.6 driving a GaAs LED.
3) Be sure to use a photodiode that is in a package proof against visible light. But note that this will not prevent the IR component of visible light sources interfering with operation.
4) Use a circuit such as Figure 2.7 which has a trigger action.
5) Use a system based on tuning both transmitter and receiver to a fixed pulse rate (see Chapter 3).

In this circuit the photodiode is reverse-biased so that only a small leakage current flows through it. The size of the leakage current depends on the amount of IR falling on the diode. The small current flowing through the relatively large resistor R1 generates an appreciable potential across it, the potential depending upon the amount of IR. When no IR is being received, there is a small potential across R1 and this is not high enough to turn Q1 on. The circuit is a Schmitt trigger. A small rise of potential across R1 turns Q1 on and Q2 off, making the output of the circuit rise to +6V. Once the circuit is triggered, its state can not be reversed by reducing the IR slightly. It requires an appreciable fall in IR to turn Q1 off again and turn Q2 on again. After that, the IR must rise appreciably before the state of the circuit is again reversed. This 'snap action' gives the circuit a rapid response to significant changes in IR, while making it immune to small changes caused by other sources of IR in the vicinity. VR1 adjusts the bias to Q1, so controlling the level at which switching occurs.

Output switching
The output of Figure 2.7 may connected to logic circuits for further processing of the signal, as in Chapter 3. In single-pulse systems the output is more often used to control a relay, a low-voltage motor, a lamp or some other load directly. The principle of switching is more-or-less the same for all types of load that operate on DC. Loads can be switched by using a bipolar junction transistor (BJT) but MOSFETs are more generally suitable. See Chapter 5 for more details on device driving.

A cable system

Perhaps an electric door-bell is the most common and elementary form of remote control possible. The input interface (the push-button) is linked directly to the controlled device (the bell) by a pair of wires. It might be considered that such a system hardly ranks as remote control. But a slight variation on this, in which a push-button remotely activates a relay, which in turn switches on a mains-powered electric motor, is much closer to the idea of remote control. The signal is sent at low voltage and low current, yet the motor operates at high voltage and with high current. This is a much safer technique than switching the motor directly through a cable carrying the mains supply.

When we come to activating multiple-pulse coders and PPM devices through a cable, we are well into the realm of remote control. At this point certain problems may arise, particularly if the cable is long. The output terminals of logic and other ics are not designed for passing signals into long cables. The cable offers impedance to signals, particularly high-frequency pulses. When a pulse changes level from low to high or from high to low, this is a rapid change so that, even if the pulses are transmitted slowly, their sharp rises and falls become distorted and the pulses lose their 'square' shape. In a system which relies on detecting the beginnings and ends of the pulse this is an even more serious matter. In addition, the longer the line the greater amount of electromagnetic interference (EMI) that is picked up.

Electromagnetic interference can be reduced by using shielded cable, with the shielding connected to the 0V line of the equipment either in the transmitter or in the receiver. However, over short distances, a twisted pair of wires is often sufficiently immune to interference. EMI affects both wires more-or-less equally; we say that the interference is *common-mode*. What matters is the potential difference between the wires instant by instant and this remains unaffected if *both* wires are subject to rises and falls of potential.

When you are setting up a system intended for cable connection, first try connecting the transmitter and receiver by a twisted pair of wires. If this works satisfactorily, there is no need to consider improving the system. Any major source of EMI, such as pulses produced by heavy switching in nearby equipment will generally show up as occasional errors in the received signals. Once identified, the problem can be remedied by shielding.

To improve the quality of transmission, particularly that of high-frequency transmission, terminate the cable at the transmitter end with a line driver and at the receiver end with a line receiver. The 14C88 and 14C89 are an easy-to-use pair of ics (Fig. 2.8). Each contains four gates, which can therefore service 4 independent transmission lines.

In the 14C88 line driver (IC1 of Fig. 2.8) three of the gates are NAND gates, which allows for logical operations such as enabling and disabling them under logical control. Normally they are used with their inputs joined together, so that they act as INVERT gates. The fourth gate in IC1 is an INVERT gate. The gate receives input from TTL or CMOS (including 74HC00 series). It requires a dual power supply but has the flexibility of being able to run on any voltage from ±4.5V to ±12.5V. The negative supply can be obtained by using a 7660 voltage converter ic (Fig. 2.9, D1 is required only when +V is 6.5V or more) if it is not available from other sources. The output signal is symmetrical about 0V, and depends on the power supply, being ±3V for a ±4.5V supply, ±7V for a ±9V supply or ±9V for a ±12V supply. This CMOS version does not

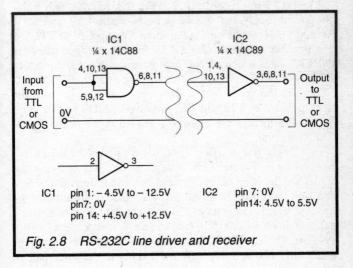

Fig. 2.8   RS-232C line driver and receiver

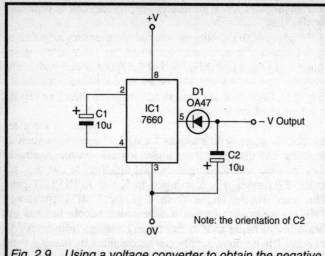

Fig. 2.9   Using a voltage converter to obtain the negative
voltage for a dual supply.

require a capacitor at its output, as did the earlier non-CMOS
version.

The 14C89 line receiver (IC2 in Fig. 2.8) requires only a single power supply but this must be between 4.5V and 5.5V.
Normally this would run on the usual 5V supplied to TTL but
it is possible to run it from a 4.5V battery. All four gates are
INVERT gates which accept input from the driver and produce
a TTL or CMOS compatible output. Since the signal is inverted both in the driver and in the receiver, it emerges with the
same polarity as it began. This improved CMOS version does
not require the control capacitors needed in the original non-
CMOS version.

For longer transmission lines, use a differential driver and
receiver as in Figure 2.10. Instead of one line carrying the
signal and the other being a ground line, in a differential system
one line transmits the signal and the other line transmits the
inverted signal. The gates of IC1 are to be connected to separate
pairs of lines so that IC1 can service 4 independent control
systems, 4 pairs of lines. Sometimes it is convenient to connect
gates from two or more *different* 75172s to the *same* pair of

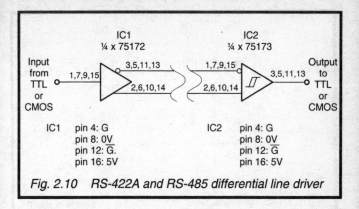

Fig. 2.10   RS-422A and RS-485 differential line driver

lines so that two signals may be transmitted along the same pair of lines. This is the most economical thing to do if the distance is great. Then we arrange that only one gate is connected to the lines at any given instant and that all other gates have their outputs in a high-impedance state. If the G input (pin 4) is made high or the G-bar input (pin 12) is made low, all gates in the ic are enabled. To disable the outputs make input G low and input G-bar high. This applies also to the 75173 so that outputs from several *different* 75173s can be connected to the same computer bus. If you do not wish to make use of this facility, and simply have the gates permanently enabled, connect both G and G-bar to the 0V line of the transmitter and receiver circuits.

A similar pair of devices are the 75174 line driver and 74175 line receiver. The two enabling inputs are both active-high, the one at pin 4 controlling gates 1 and 2 (the lower pin numbers) and the other at pin 12 controlling gates 3 and 4 (the higher pin numbers). As an example of the many possibilities Figure 2.11 shows how to use one cable for two independent signal channels. Only one of pins 4 and 12 must be made high at the same time. This driver, and also the 75173 have built-in *contention protection*, which means that they shut down if, by accident, two or more drivers become connected to the line at the same time and cause over-loading of the ics.

In certain systems it is necessary to provide for a feedback signal to indicate whether or not the desired action has occurred. A sensor or other deive which is part of the controlled device

31

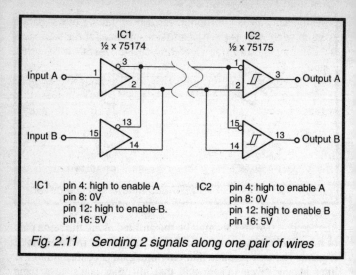

IC1
½ x 75174

IC2
½ x 75175

Input A o——1 ▷ 3
2

1 ◁ 3 o—— Output A
2

Input B o——15 ▷ 13
14

15 ◁ 13 o—— Output B
14

IC1 pin 4: high to enable A
pin 8: 0V
pin 12: high to enable B.
pin 16: 5V

IC2 pin 4: high to enable A
pin 8: 0V
pin 12: high to enable B
pin 16: 5V

Fig. 2.11   Sending 2 signals along one pair of wires

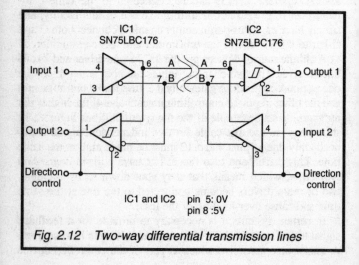

IC1
SN75LBC176

IC2
SN75LBC176

Input 1 o——4 ▷ 6 A   A 6 ◁ 1 o—— Output 1
3   7 B   B 7   2

Output 2 o——1 ◁
2

4 ▷ o—— Input 2
3

Direction o
control

o Direction
control

IC1 and IC2   pin 5: 0V
pin 8 :5V

Fig. 2.12   Two-way differential transmission lines

32

signals back to the transmitter. Instead of having two separate pairs of wires, one of the transmission and one for the feedback, we can employ two-way signalling on the same pair of wires. Figure 2.12 shows how to use a pair of ics, each of which contains a driver and a receiver. This is differential signalling so is suitable for longer distances. At each end we need a 5V regulated power supply and the necessary logic to enable driving or receiving. If the control input is high, this enables the driver; when it goes low, the receiver is enabled. Logic circuits are required at both ends to switch the control input.

The cost of the cable is often a major consideration. If the system needs to be expanded later, the cost of laying new cable increases the overall cost of the system still further. Then it is best to use multiple-channel techniques, such as dividing the signals into subsets, using address-coded signals (as described in Chapter 3), or wiring several drivers on to the same pair of lines (as described in the previous paragraph). The system is expandable with no additional costs for cable.

A radio system

This system is based on the TXM-418-A transmitter module and the SILRX-418-A receiver module, manufactured by Radiometrix. It is generally a simple matter to adapt these ideas to other ready-made transmitters and receivers. This is a frequency-modulated system. The modules are on small circuit boards, measuring 30mm × 9.5mm for the transmitter and 48mm × 21mm for the receiver. They have a single-in-line pinout, so they can conveniently be mounted on the project circuit board in a standard 2.54mm single-in-line socket. Or they can be soldered directly to the board, and are suitable for mounting on standard stripboard. On each module, the two radio-frequency pins are isolated at one end of the board, while power connections and data input/output pins are in a group at the other end (Fig. 2.13).

Transmitter

The operating voltage of the transmitter is between 6V and 12V; that of the receiver is between 4.5V and 9V. These levels are entirely suitable for battery operation. Since current

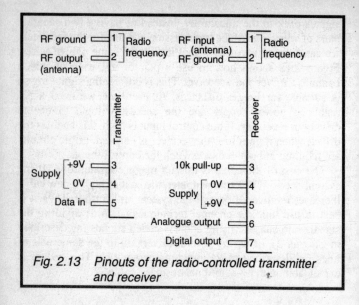

Fig. 2.13   Pinouts of the radio-controlled transmitter and receiver

requirements are only 10 or so milliamps, it is feasible to use a 9V PP3 battery in projects where small battery size is an asset.

The modules each require an antenna, which can be purchased ready-made. The most suitable is a quarter-wavelength (150mm) flexible whip antenna, though a quarter wavelength helical stub antenna is more compact. It is also possible to obtain a 5/8-wavelength whip antenna which has 3dB (double power) gain. This give an increase in range, or more reliable communication in noisy conditions, but the regulations allow this to be fitted only to the receiver. A home-made whip antenna may take the form of a straight wire or rod 16.5cm long. Preferably this should project from the top of the casing. If an internal antenna is necessary for any reason, an alternative is a straight pcb track of the same length. Or use a combination of wire/rod and track totalling 16.5cm. A helical antenna is made by taking a former 3.5mm in diameter and winding 34 turns of 0.5mm diameter enamelled copper wire around it with adjacent turns touching. In each case the antenna is permanently connected. This takes up less space than the whip antenna but its performance is not as good. When positioning the antenna, remember to leave space around it and not to place it close to large metal components or to parts of the circuit which generate radio-frequency interference, such as microcontrollers and logic ics. While the antenna of the transmitter must be integral with the module, it is permitted to use an external antenna with the receiver, connected to the module by coaxial cable.

The transmission range is naturally much greater in the open than in a building. Range is greater when both transmitter and receiver are a metre or more above ground level. Indoors, a partition wall made from wall-board mounted on a timber frame absorbs relatively small amounts of the signal. Walls made from brick and similar materials absorb more, concrete reinforced with a metal grid absorbs even more and a wholly metal wall (such as a metal garden shed) prevents signals passing altogether. Other large objects made from metal, for example steel shelving, can also interfere with transmission. Factors of this sort must be taken into account when positioning the transmitter and receiver, unless a range of only a few metres is required.

As far as the projects in this book are concerned we are dealing only with transmission of pulses, that is to say, logic levels. The signal may be one that changes from low to high so infrequently that it rates as a DC signal. At the other extreme, the system can handle pulses as short as 100μs. The input to the receiver is controlled by a push-button or fed from the output of a CMOS buffer or gate, or a MOSFET switching circuit operating on the same power supply. This means that most of the control circuits described in this book may be connected directly to the transmitter input. Figure 3.3 and Figure 3.4 may be used for simple push-button control when de-bouncing is required. A single pulse or a series of pulses is registered by all 418MHz receivers within the local reception area. This may lead to problems if there is more than one receiver in range. With ordinary radio control, such as when members of a model aeroplane club have several craft in the air at once, we get over this difficulty by transmitting on a slightly different wavelength (frequency) for each model. Transmitters have plug-in crystals to tune the circuit effortlessly, with corresponding crystals plugged into the receivers. With the system described here, only one frequency is permitted so we have to adopt other means to ensure that a signal is responded to by the intended receiver and no others. The solution is to use a coder such as the MV500 (Fig. 3.18 and Fig. 3.19) or the MC145026 (Fig. 3.21). Coders are run from the same power supply as the transmitter and the output terminal of the coder is connected directly to pin 5 of the transmitter.

Receiver

At the receiver, an appropriate decoder (MV601 or MC145027, for example) with its input connected directly to the output of the receiver module, recognises the coded signal and responds if the codes match. In this way hundreds of transmitter-receiver pairs can be operated in the same neighbourhood with utmost security. It is also possible for a single transmitter to control several selected receivers simultaneously, or for a single receiver to be controllable by several transmitters.

Regulations

The following are the more important requirements:

1 The transmitter antenna must be integral with the module, that is permanently and directly connected to the module, without an external feeder.
2 The transmitter antenna must be not be of a type which provides gain.
3 The trimmer control on both transmitter and receiver must never be adjusted. It must be inaccessible when the module is finally enclosed in its box.
4 The case of the transmitter must have a label clearly visible on its outside. The label must be at least 10mm × 15mm, bearing a message 'MPT 1340 W.T. LICENCE EXEMPT', in characters at least 2mm high.

Projects

Below we describe some projects that make use of the single-pulse systems described in this chapter. Although each project is aimed at a specific application, you will find it easy to adapt the projects to a very wide range of other applications. For explanations of the output/driving sections of the circuits you may need to look ahead to Chapter 5, where all the many output possibilities are described. This is a book about electronic aspects of remote control; the mechanical details of projects are given in outline only and much of this side of the project is left to the ingenuity and skill of the reader. In many cases, mechanical problems can be reduced by using ready-made mechanisms. For example where we refer to a 'model vehicle' this may be one that you have designed and built entirely from scratch, or it may be one you have built using a constructional set, or you may have bought a factory assembled model and simply need to incorporate the control circuits.

Project 1 – Remote Control for a Model Vehicle

This is an example of single-pulse control using ultrasound. In essence, it is a remotely controlled relay and can be used to switch on and off almost any battery-powered equipment. If it is used with a model vehicle such as a tank, the tank moves for as long as the transmitter button is pressed and stops when the button is released. Project 1 can also be used with boats, electrically-powered talking dolls and many other electronic novelty toys.

The transmitter is the unit described in Figure 2.1. The receiver is as described in Figure 2.2, modified as in Figure 2.3 for switching a relay. The relay can be almost any normally-open relay. Figure 2.14 shows the connections. The circuit-board should be made small enough to conceal within the model, with the crystal suitably exposed - either on the board itself or mounted separately on the outside of the model with a pair of wires connecting it to the circuit board. Assuming that the model has a 6V, 9V or 12V battery supply, this is connected to the circuit board. The positive line is connected to the far side of the model's own switch so that turning this off interrupts the supply both to the receiver circuit board and the model's motor or other circuit. The positive lead joining the model's switch to the motor is cut where shown.

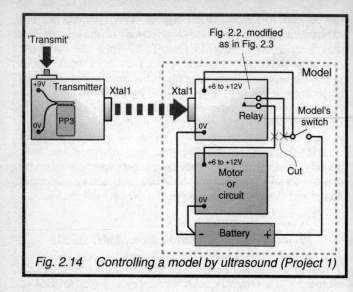

Fig. 2.14   Controlling a model by ultrasound (Project 1)

Warning:
If the model or equipment is still under manufacturer's guarantee, the guarantee may be invalidated by cutting the wire.

The relay contacts are wired to either side of the cut. The relay may be any small sort with normally-open contacts. Provided that it is rated for the current taken by the model (you should measure this with a test-meter before buying the relay) a reed relay (in ic-style case) or a subminiature or miniature pcb-mounting type is suitable (see Chapter 5). A relay with changeover contacts (SPDT) may be used instead of the SPST type shown in the figure.

It may happen with certain models that the motor or other circuitry of the model generates so much interference on the power supply lines that the receiver fails to work reliably. It may be possible to cure this by increasing the value of C1 to 470µF, or even more. If this produces no improvement, provide a separate battery for the receiver.

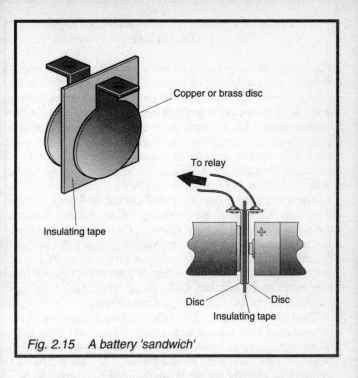

Fig. 2.15   A battery 'sandwich'

If you do not wish to interfere with the wiring of the model
by cutting one of its leads use a battery sandwich. This consists
of two metal discs with a layer of insulating tape between them
(Fig. 2.15). This is inserted between two of the cells in the
battery compartment. If you use a battery sandwich, you will
need to provide a separate battery supply for the receiver board.

Project 2 – Remotely Controlled Porch Light
– DC Version

Particularly if the porch is an the shady side of the house at night, it gives a feeling of security if the porch light can be switched on when you reach the garden gate. External wiring from the gateway to the porch is rarely practicable or safe, but remote control has no such limitations. This circuit can also control a garage light, a bedside lamp, or a light for a dark corridor. This version operates on batteries, so is entirely safe to construct. Pressing the button of the remote control turns the lamp on. It then stays on automatically for a preset period.

The transmitter is one of those illustrated in Figure 2.5, the number of LEDs required depending on the distance between the porch and the gate. Use GaAs LEDs to extend the range. For maximum range, use the high-intensity flashing circuit of Figure 2.6. Since the porch is on the dark side of the house, there will probably be no interference from street lighting. You may find that the headlamps of passing cars occasionally trigger the receiver, but this is no great disadvantage.

The receiver is Figure 2.7. The switching circuit (Fig. 2.16) is based on a 7555 timer which is triggered by a *low* pulse to its input (pin 2). So that this can be triggered by the usual *high* pulse from the receiver, we use a transistor Q1 and resistor R1 to invert the receiver output. When the 7555 is triggered its output (pin 3) goes high for a period determined by the values of R2 and C1. The 'on' time is given by:

$$t = 0.69 \times R2 \times C1$$

For example, if R2 = 1MΩ and C1 = 100μF, then the lamp is on for nearly 70 seconds, which would be ample time in which to walk up to the door and unlock it.

The choice of lamp requires some thought. Tungsten halogen filament lamps are available rated at 4.4W and running on a 5.2V supply. Allowing for the voltage drop across the switching transistor, these would give their maximum light output with a supply voltage of 6V. For greater illumination, use a 10W tungsten halogen lamp running on 12V. Low-voltage filament lamps of the type used in motor vehicles could also

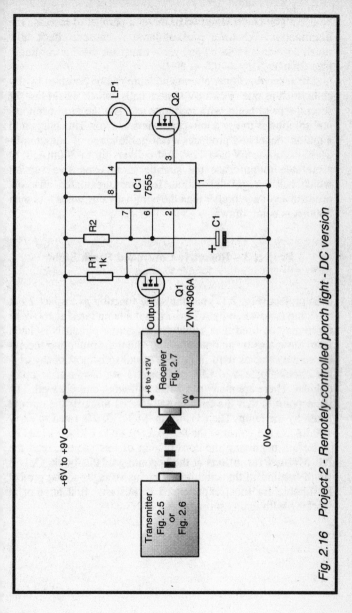

Fig. 2.16 Project 2 - Remotely-controlled porch light - DC version

41

be used; you could wire two or three in parallel to increase the illumination. Whatever type of lamp is chosen, check how much current is required and use a transistor rated accordingly (see Chapter 5).

The receiver, trigger circuit and lamp can be powered by dry cells, such as one or two 6V lantern cells, which would last for several tens of hours with moderate use. But the most economical solution is to use a low-cost mains adaptor. This plugs into a mains socket and produces a selectable range of output voltages, including 6V and 12V, and delivers up to 300mA. It is preferable to purchase the slightly more expensive version which has a regulated output, for the unregulated adaptors produce a voltage higher than the nominal value when less than 300mA is being drawn.

Project 3 – Remotely Controlled Porch Light
– AC Version

This project (Fig. 2.17) has the same function as Project 2 but the lamp is powered by AC mains, and a lamp rated at 100W or more may be used. For safety the triggering circuit is isolated from the mains by an opto-coupler. The transmitter and receiver are the same as used in Project 2, and so is most of the trigger circuit. Instead of LP1 of Project 2 we have a triac opto-coupler. There are many types that will work equally well. The main point is that the triac must be rated to carry the current taken by the lamp. The triac of the MOC3020 is rated to carry 100mA, so the power of the lamp can be up to $230 \times 0.1 = 23$W.

Before beginning the construction of this project, read the **AC Mains Precautions** at the beginning of this book. Only a small fraction of this circuit is at mains voltages so the project is suitable for most experienced enthusiasts' first attempt at working with mains supplies.

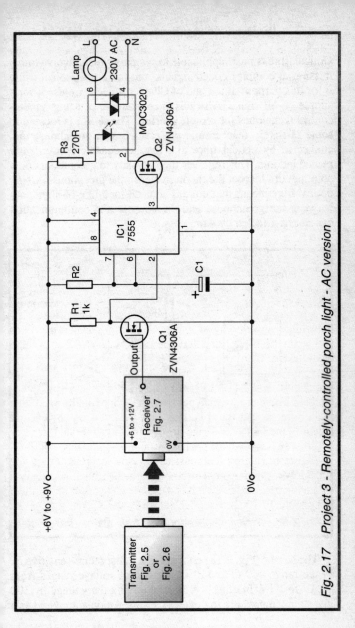

Fig. 2.17   Project 3 - Remotely-controlled porch light - AC version

43

Project 4 – Greenhouse Frost Warning

Optical fibre is more applicable to systems which involve transmission of complex coded signals, and there is a project using
it for this purpose at the end of Chapter 4. Here we use it for a
simple on-off signal. Also this is an example of using remote-
control techniques for remote sensing. The sensor is located in
some relatively inaccessible place, such as a greenhouse and
connected by optical fibre to a display console conveniently
placed indoors. This removes the necessity to go outdoors on a
cold night to inspect the thermometer in the greenhouse. Using
optical fibre means that there is no need for a line-of-sight path
between the greenhouse and the console and communication
can not be affected by dampness.

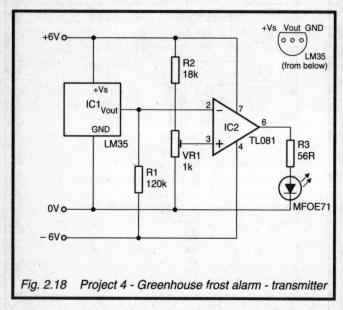

Fig. 2.18   Project 4 - Greenhouse frost alarm - transmitter

The sensor (Fig. 2.18) consists of a temperature-sensitive ic.
In the range –40°C to 110°C, the output voltage ranges from
–0.4V to 1.1V. In other words, multiplying the voltage by 100
gives the temperature in degrees Celsius. An op amp wired as a

comparator is set to give a high output when the temperature falls below a preset level. A cermet trimmer is recommended for VR1. The high level switches on an LED. Here we specify a fibre optic sender which takes a current of 100mA. It may be necessary to alter R3 with other senders. The light from the sender travels by optical fibre to the display console. In the console, the light from the fibre is detected by a fibre optic detector (MF0D71), which contains a phototransistor. The simple receiver circuit of Figure 2.7 is adequate, with the detector wired in place of D1. The easiest way to obtain an effective output from this is to wire a *flashing* LED in place of R4. Flashing LEDs operate on a 6V supply and include the circuitry needed to produce the flashing; they operate on the full supply voltage (3.5 – 13V) and do not require a resistor in series with them. If you wish, an 'electronic buzzer' can be wired in parallel with the LED to supply audible warning.

The –6V supply to the sensor may be provided by a battery or by a 7660 voltage converter (Fig. 2.9). The values of R2 and VR1 allow the wiper of VR1 to be set at any voltage between 0V (= 0°C) and 0.3V (= 30°C). Adjust VR1 until the voltage at its wiper is that corresponding to the temperature below which the alarm is to be activated. It is easy to modify this circuit by using a MOSFET to invert the output from Figure 2.7. Then the LED flashes when the temperature *exceeds* a given value, so converting the system into an overheating warning device.

The sensor ic could be replaced by a circuit based on a thermistor, but we have chosen to use the ic partly because it makes it easier to set the temperature level and partly because it is simpler to convert the circuit at a later date so that the display console has a numeric display of the temperature in degrees.

Project 5 – Radio Pager

This is one of the simplest of radio-controlled projects, and can also be adapted as a cordless doorbell. The price of its simplicity is that it is not selective. The pager may respond to any 418MHz transmitter within range and the transmitter may interfere with other 418MHz systems in the vicinity. If this is unacceptable, build the coded system described in Chapter 3, Project 11.

The transmitter (Fig. 2.19) is switched on when button S1 is pressed. Its data input is wired permanently to the positive supply so it transmits a 'high' signal as soon as it is switched on. The circuit is mounted in a hand-held enclosure; several different designs of ready-made remote control enclosure are available. The circuit is best powered by a 9V PP3 battery but, if you have an enclosure with a built-in battery compartment,

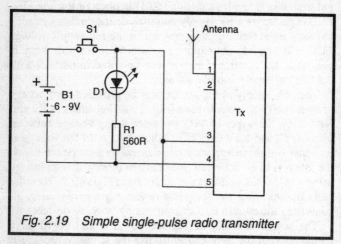

Fig. 2.19   Simple single-pulse radio transmitter

the transmitter may be powered by four AA cells. The LED is an optional but useful addition to the circuit, confirming that a signal has been sent and also acting as a battery freshness indication. If using a 6V supply, reduce R1 to 390Ω. For a more compact transmitter use a pair of 3V lithium manganese cells, mounted in retainer clips and connected in series. For example, CR2016 cells are 20mm in diameter and have a capacity of 72mAh. A pair will last about 4 hours in total, equivalent to over 16000 one-second pulses. For short-range transmission and for the most compact controller it is preferable to use a helical antenna, mounted directly on the circuit board. Whatever the antenna type, its connection to the transmitter module must be as short as possible.

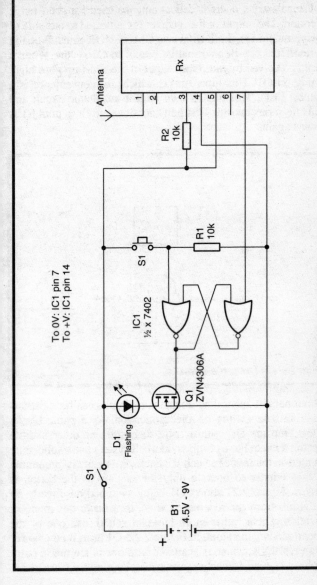

Fig. 2.20   Simple single-pulse radio-pager receiver

47

The receiver (Fig. 2.20) is likewise be mounted in a small enclosure and an internal helical antenna used for short-range reception. The output of the receiver is connected to one side of a set-reset flip-flop built from two CMOS NOR gates. Pressing S1 resets the flip-flop so that its output to Q1 is low. When a pulse is received by radio the output of the flip-flop goes high, turning on Q1. This turns on D1 which, for convenience is a flashing LED. This has its own built-in oscillator circuit and needs no series resistor. The LED continues to flash until S1 is pressed again.

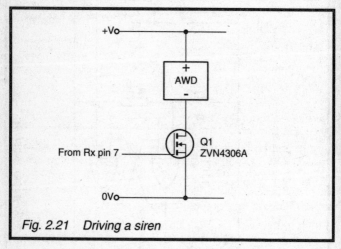

Fig. 2.21   Driving a siren

Innumerable other devices and sub-circuits can be substituted for D1, depending on the application. As a panic button system, replace D1 with a solid-state siren or other audible warning device. For a cordless doorbell system use a solid-state sounder or 'buzzer'. In such a system, it is usually preferable for the sounder to operate only for as long as the button is pressed. Figure 2.21 shows Q1 being switched on directly by the output from the receiver module, to achieve this mode of operation. For a rather more pleasant sound, use one of the many melody generators. In Figure 2.22, Q1 turns on the power for an H381XX, which is available with one of ten tunes, ranging from 'Greensleeves' to 'We wish you a merry Christmas'.

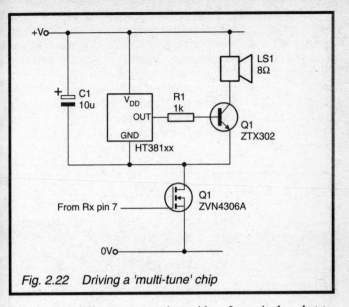

Fig. 2.22   Driving a 'multi-tune' chip

Buy several different ones and provide a 3-terminal socket to
that you can change the tune to suit the season. If you have a
strong sense of humour, you may like to use a sound-effects
generator instead; the sound of a police car or an aeroplane is
heard whenever the door-bell button is pressed.

Chapter 3

SIGNALS

In Chapter 2 we have considered systems operating in a binary, single-pulse or on-off mode. Usually the transmitter has a push button, which is either pressed or released. A pulse of ultra-sound, infra-red, or current passes from the transmitter to the receiver. The output of the receiver goes high or low and switches a load (such as a motor) on or off. This is the most basic remote control system. Even though it is simple, it has many applications.

Sequential Systems

The next more complicated system is the sequential system in which successive pulses produce a sequence of different results. Only one step up from the single-pulse response is the two-pulse toggle response. As an example, take a porch-light control in which the first pulse turns the lamp on and the second one turns it off. Controlling a motor in a model tank, the first pulse starts the tank moving and the second pulse stops it. It stops and starts alternately as successive pulses are received.

Figure 3.1 is the circuit module that produces toggle action. It is a J-K flip-flop that can easily be added to the ultrasound receiver of Figure 2.2. Just wire the output of Figure 2.2 to the input of Figure 3.1. Then the output of Figure 3.1 is connected to a MOSFET switch (Chapter 5) to drive a load. The input of the toggle unit can also be connected to the output of the infra-red receiver of Figure 2.7, or to the line receivers of Figures 2.8, 2.10, 2.11 or 2.12. Connect the other pins of IC1 to 0V or the positive supply line as indicated in Figure 3.1. This is a CMOS ic and works on any supply voltage (+V) from 3V to 15V, and need not be regulated. The same applies to other CMOS circuits described in this chapter. The 4027B ic contains two identical J-K flip-flops, so it can serve two receivers. If only one of the flip-flops is used, connect the clock input pin of the unused one to 0V or +V.

The J-K flip-flop has some features that can extend its possible applications. It has an alternative output, the Q-bar

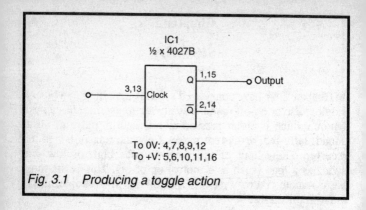

Q 1,15 o Output

3,13 Clock

Q̄ 2,14

To 0V: 4,7,8,9,12
To +V: 5,6,10,11,16

Fig. 3.1   Producing a toggle action

output. The output at this pin is always the inverse on the output at the Q pin. This allows you to control two devices, turning one off when you turn the other on. Or you can control two functions on the same device as long as only one at a time is supposed to be switched on. The Q bar output is also useful when the circuit to be turned on requires a low input to do so.

Four of the terminals which are wired to 0V in Figure 3.1 are actually direct set and reset inputs. When made high they either set (Q goes high, Q-bar goes low) or reset (Q goes low, Q-bar goes high) the flip-flop. This happens immediately and is independent of the input to the circuit. In Figure 3.2 we see how to use these inputs to set or reset the latch by means of push-buttons *on the controlled device*, not by remote control. If you need only the setting or resetting function, omit the push-button on the other input and connect it permanently to 0V.

De-bouncing

One of the problems that may arise with any circuit more complicated than the single-pulse circuits of Chapter 2 is that what appears to be a single pulse may in fact be a series of many pulses. When a switch or push-button is closed, the metal contacts may touch and separate many times before they *finally* close together. Conversely, when the push-button is released or the switch opens, the contacts may come apart and close again several times before they *finally* open. This is known as *contact bounce*. The result is a series of short

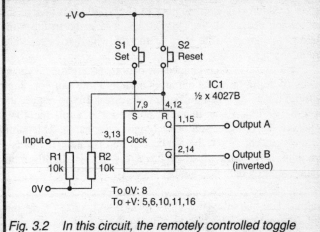

*Fig. 3.2   In this circuit, the remotely controlled toggle
action is overridden by set and reset buttons*

unintended pulses at the beginning and end of the longer
(intended) pulse. The short pulses may follow each other so
quickly that the intended pulse appears to begin and end clean-
ly. By looking at, say, the indicator LED D1 in Figure 2.6 we
are unable to detect these multiple pulses. But a logic circuit
works fast and, in the case of the toggle circuit, changes state at

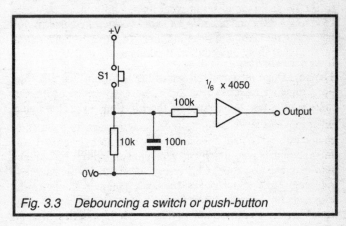

Fig. 3.3   Debouncing a switch or push-button

53

each short pulse. By chance, pressing the button generates either an odd or an even number of short pulses so that, at the end of the operation, the toggled device may be in the same state or in the opposite state to that in which it began. The control system breaks down.

The solution is to de-bounce the button and Figure 3.3 shows a way of doing this. The output is normally low and goes high without bouncing when the button is pressed. If you require the opposite action, use an inverting buffer, for example the 4049. It takes time for the capacitor to charge or discharge, which limits the speed at which the button can be operated. If this is a problem, use the circuit of Figure 3.4, which is slightly more elaborate but which acts almost instantly.

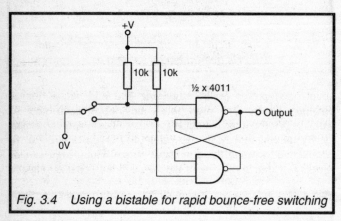

Fig. 3.4   Using a bistable for rapid bounce-free switching

Longer Sequences
The next stage in sequential signalling is to join two J-K flip-flops together in series (Fig. 3.5). Successive pulses from the transmitter cause the outputs of the flip-flops to go through a four-stage sequence:

Stage No.	Output ff1	Output ff2
0	Low	Low
1	High	Low
2	Low	High
3	High	High

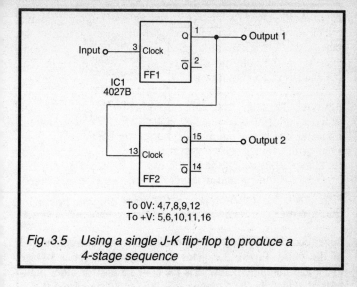

*Fig. 3.5   Using a single J-K flip-flop to produce a
4-stage sequence*

What use can be made of this depends on the application. It
controls just two functions, for example a model vehicle may
have its motor controlled by flip-flop 1 and its headlights controlled by flip-flop 2. We can obtain all possible combinations
of stop/start and lights on/off by cycling through the sequence.
If the vehicle is motionless with its light off (stage 0) and we
want it go begin moving with its lights on (stage 2), we send
two pulses in quick succession so that it is only momentarily in
stage 1.

The number of flip-flops in the array can be extended almost
indefinitely. But when we reach more than about 8 stages, skipping unwanted stages becomes cumbersome and it is better to
use one of the systems described later in this chapter. For up to
about 8 stages it is simpler to use a counter ic rather than an
array of flip-flops (Fig. 3.6). The counters contain virtually the
same flip-flops already connected. There are several CMOS
counters that can be used but the 4020 is not likely to be help-
ful for its lacks outputs from stages 2 and 3. The 4024B in
Figure 3.6 in fact allows you to have a 128-stage programme,
though the situation in which you would want to do this would
be extremely unusual. The 4024B changes state on a falling

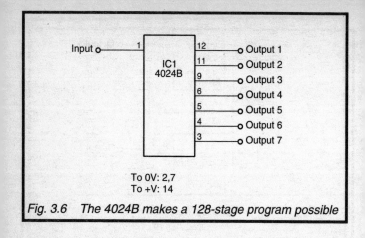

Fig. 3.6   The 4024B makes a 128-stage program possible

edge; you send a pulse and the counter changes state at the end of the pulse. Figure 3.7 gives the connections for a 5-stage cycle and the table below lists the connections for other numbers of stages. In the 5-stage cycle the output runs from 0 to 4 then, as it changes to count 5, with outputs 1 and 3 both high, the logic gate gates instantly detect this state and reset the counter to 0. The count of 5 is extremely short-lived and would not be noticed normally. The counter resets when a high level is applied to pin 2 so we really need an AND gate taking its inputs from outputs 1 and 3. If your circuit has an AND gate to spare you can use this. Take its output directly to pin 2 of IC1. But it is more likely that you will have NAND gates. Two of these are used as in Figure 3.7, the first performing the logic and the second simply inverting the result. For other numbers of stages you can use either a direct connection to pin 2, or AND (usually NAND plus INVERT as in Fig. 3.7) two or three outputs:

No. of stages	Output(s) to pin 2
3	1 AND 2
4	3
5	1 AND 3
6	2 AND 3
7	1 AND 2 AND 3
8	4

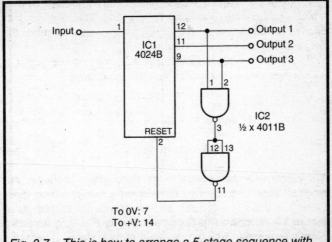

Fig. 3.7   This is how to arrange a 5-stage sequence with
the 4024B

In general, the type of switching described above allows us to produce different *combinations* of actions. It is very useful for controlling vehicles in which, for example, we may wish to control motion by switching the motor on and off and *at the same time* (yet independently) control the headlamps, switching them on or off whether the vehicle is in motion or not. There are four combinations and all may be obtained by a sequence of four output stages. When we have three or more flip-flops in series, or a counter as in Figure 3.6 it becomes more difficult to merely use the outputs to switch things on or off. For example, consider a 4-stage counter controlling four functions in a model vehicle. There are 16 possible combinations:

No.	Motor	Headlamp	Interior lights	Hooter
0	Off	Off	Off	Off
1	Off	Off	Off	On
2	Off	Off	On	Off
3	Off	Off	On	On

and so on to...

| 15 | On | On | On | On |

It is going to require some mental agility to decide exactly which combination you want at any one time. We need to *decode* the outputs from the flip-flops or counter to make the decisions for us.

The simplest type of decoding switches on just *one output at a time*. For example, a model boat has 4 functions:

> 0   stop
> 1   motor forward
> 2   motor backward
> 3   sound foghorn

There are, of course, several ways of designing the logic, but we shall look at a standard technique for one-at-a-time functions. The basis is a counter, and we decode the outputs as in Figure 3.8. The two flip-flops (wired as in Fig. 3.5) have two output terminals, which give four output *states*. These are decoded by the NOR gates of IC2 to make the four output terminals go high one at a time:

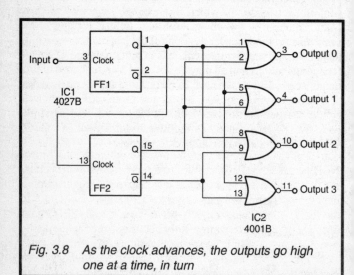

Fig. 3.8   As the clock advances, the outputs go high
one at a time, in turn

Stage 0 is a no-action stage in the program listed above, so there is actually no need for the gate and its connections. But, it could be used for a function appropriate to a stationary boat. For example, you could invert output 0 to switch on navigation lights when the boat is moving and to switch them *off* when it is stationary.

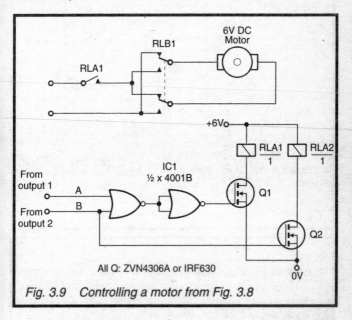

Fig. 3.9   Controlling a motor from Fig. 3.8

Stages 1 and 2 control the motor. Figure 3.9 shows a generally-useful motor direction control, using relays driven by MOSFETs. When either Output 1 or Output 2 are high, the output of the first NOR gate is low; the output of the second NOR gate is high. This activates relay A, which switches on the motor. Output 2 activates relay B which reverses the direction of the current. As an alternative, Figure 3.10 shows a circuit with the same action, but using only MOSFETs. The INVERT gates of IC2 might be more conveniently obtained from the remaining two NOR gates of IC1, by wiring their inputs together.

Output 3 goes either to a relay to switch the foghorn on or, preferably, the output powers a suitable sound-effects circuit

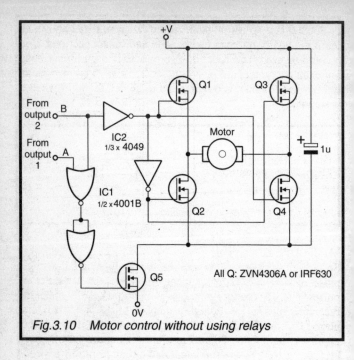

Fig.3.10   Motor control without using relays

directly.

Instead of the individual flip-flops in Figure 3.8, we could use a 4024B counter (Fig. 3.6 with output 3 connected to pin 2, to make a 4-stage counter. Note that in this type of circuit the function is active only for as long as the output is high.

Longer sequences complete with one-at-a-time decoding are obtainable by using a divide-by-10 Johnson counter (Fig. 3.11). This has 10 outputs out of which only one is high at any stage. The high output steps around the 10 output terminals at each rising edge of the clock input. If fewer than 10 different outputs are required, the counter is made to reset by a logic circuit of the kind shown in Figure 3.12. The connections to IC2 are taken from output 0 and from one of outputs 1 to 9 depending on the stage at which resetting is to occur. An example of the use of this circuit is Project 8, at the end of this chapter.

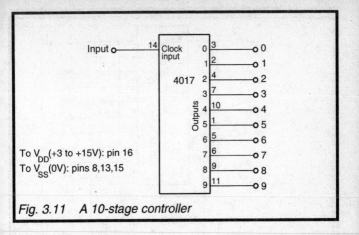

Fig. 3.11   A 10-stage controller

Multiple Pulse Control

So far in this chapter all control has been by means of a single
pulse or a sequence of identical pulses. In the sequence of
pulses, only the *number* of pulses is important. They make the
receiver circuit cycle through a number of distinct states, lin-
gering on some and quickly skipping though others. Another
approach, one which is used in almost all commercially-built
systems, is to use a special integrated circuit to produce a code
sequence. The signal is then transmitted by ultra-sound, cable,
IR or radio. After its detection by the receiver it is decoded by
another special-purpose integrated circuit. In this chapter we
describe two popular systems. One of these uses the MV500
coder and the MV601 decoder. The other system is based on the
MC145026 or similar coder.

MV500 PPM coder

The MV500 coder has a 32-key input which generates 32 five-
bit codes from 00000 to 11111. The coding scheme is known as
pulse position modulation (PPM) and is based on a train of six
pulses. The pulses are short and of constant length. It is the
interval *between* pulses that conveys the information. A short
interval indicates a '1', a longer interval indicates a '0' and an
even longer interval (S) terminates the group of pulses. The
code group is repeated for as long as the key is held down. If

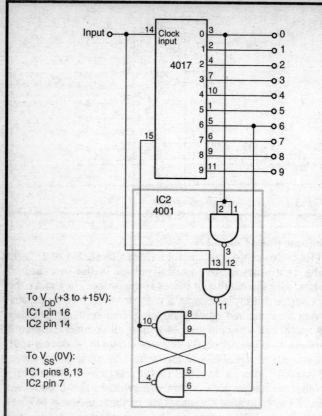

Fig. 3.12   A CMOS counter-decoder connected to reset at the 7th count, making a 6 - stage sequence controller

the key is released in the middle of a group, the transmission continues until the end of the group.

The keys are wired to a matrix (Fig. 3.13). When a key is pressed, it connects one of eight *current source* pins (pins 2-9) to one of four current *sink pins* (pins 10-13). Taking the code group to be EDCBA, we can work out the code by noting which pair of lines in Figure 3.13 has been connected. In a complete

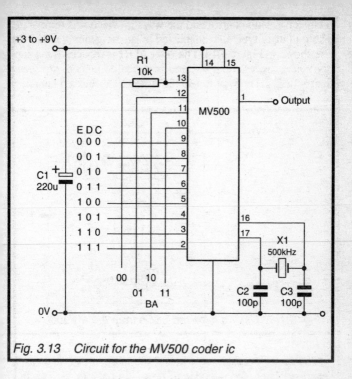

Fig. 3.13   Circuit for the MV500 coder ic

keyboard, there is a key at every intersection between the current sink lines and the current source lines. As we shall see later, there is absolutely no need for the keyboard to be complete.

The MV500 and associated circuitry is easily accommodated on a small circuit board, housed in a purpose-designed hand-held enclosure. The ic requires little power and the LED(s) operate only intermittently, so a 9V PP3 battery is ideal. Mount the keys on the panel; although up to 32 keys can be used (use a ready-made key-panel if you need such a large number of keys), it is very unlikely that you will have as many functions to control. Instead, you can mount keys and push-buttons of various shapes and colours, grouping them according to the functions they control. This means that, before you construct the transmitter, you will already have decided on the functions the receiver is to control and the ways in which it is to operate. The output is typically connected to an IR generator like the one shown in Figure 3.14. The value of R1 is reduced if the supply voltage is less than 9V, and is increased if there are fewer than 3 LEDs. The way to use the system is discussed later.

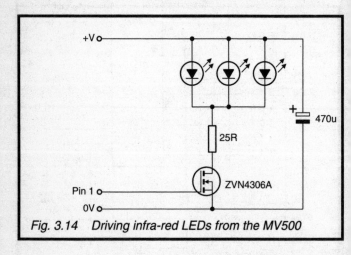

Fig. 3.14   Driving infra-red LEDs from the MV500

The coder operates at a preset modulation rate and, as is described later, the decoder ic responds only to signals that have the correct modulation rate. It is therefore a simple matter to operate two or more pairs of transmitters and receivers in the same area without any danger of interference. Just make the modulation rates sufficiently different by using matched resonators of differing frequencies. The ceramic resonator X1 (Fig. 3.13) sets the *modulation rate*, which determines the length of the '1' interval. With a 500kHz resonator as shown, the '1' interval is approximately 2ms long. Another approach is to wire the transmitter so that its modulation rate can be switched between two values., simply by switching in one of two different resonators. When wiring up the transmitter, make the connections short between pins 16/17, X1 and C2/C3, so as to minimise lead capacitance.

MV601 PPM Decoder

The MV601 (Fig. 3.15) receives and decodes signals generated by the MV500. It can also decode signals from the SL490, as described in the next section. Note that the MV601 operates on

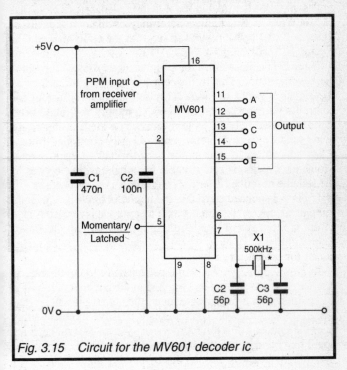

Fig. 3.15   Circuit for the MV601 decoder ic

5V, to be compatible with a wide range of logic ics. The permissible supply voltage range is 4.5V to 5.5V, so it can be powered by a 4.5V battery, if ics of the CMOS 4000 or 74HC families are used for other logic. Fig 3.15 shows the ic receiving input from a receiver amplifier such as Figures 2.8 or 2.11; there are also a number of special-purpose IR amplifier ics, such as the SL486, the TBA2800 and the TDA3047. The decoder can also receive directly from the MV500 or from a line receiver. The frequency is determined by the ceramic resonator, X1, which must have the same frequency as the resonator in the transmitter. When a signal is received, the five outputs are switched to '0' or '1' depending on the code received. These outputs can be fed to logic ics or used to drive LEDs, relays, solenoids and motors, using MOSFET switches as described earlier, and in more detail in Chapter 5. Note that certain types of ceramic resonator may oscillate at their overtones. A 220Ω resistor wired in series at the point marked * in Figure 3.15 will suppress this.

If pin 5 is connected to the positive supply line, it provides *momentary* action. That is, the code appears only for as long as the signal is being received. This action could be useful for controlling a robot or vehicle in which motors and relays need to be energised only for as long as keys on the transmitter are being held down. A 5-motor robot is easily controlled from a 5-key transmitter if one motor is connected to each output. Momentary action is also suitable for toggling flip-flops, as in the scheme described later for controlling a motor boat.

If pin 5 is connected to 0V, the action is *latched*. The code remains latched at the outputs until a new code is received. This action is more suited to controlling a radio set, tape recorder, room lighting or heating, where a given action has to be maintained for prolonged periods.

In Figure 3.15, pin 9 is wired permanently to the 0V rail. If it is wired so that it may be switched to the positive rail, or if it is provided with a 'high' logic input, the output pins all go into a high-impedance state. This makes it possible to connect this ic to the data bus of a microprocessor system. Several such ics could be connected to the bus of the Stamp, for example, and individually connected to the bus by making pin 9 high.

SL490 PPM Coder
This coder, formerly used in conjunction with the now obsolete 922 decoder, is still available from certain suppliers. It can be used instead of the MV500. It operates on 9V, but not on lower voltages as does the MV500. It has a similar keyboard circuit (Fig. 3.16) but has two outputs, operating in antiphase. Normally pin 2 is used for output. The values of C1 and R1 are used to set the length of the '1' and other intervals, so as to be equal to those expected by the decoder. With a 500kHz resonator in the MV601 the '1' interval is 2ms. To produce the

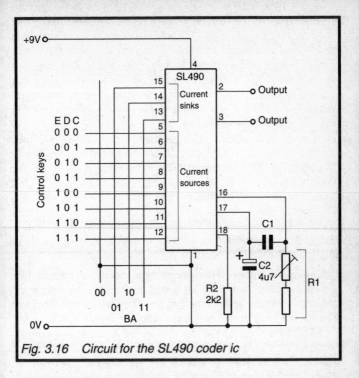

Fig. 3.16   Circuit for the SL490 coder ic

same intervals in the SL490:

$$C1 \times R1 \approx 0.0021$$

R2 should be between 15kΩ and 100kΩ. If C1 = 47nF, for
example, R1 should be about 45kΩ. Use a 36kΩ fixed resistor
in series with a 10kΩ preset potentiometer. Pin 17 is an output
which is normally low but goes high when a key is pressed.
This is used to power an LED to show that a signal is being
transmitted (Fig. 3.17).

Using the PPM System

It is rarely that all 32 different codes will be required. Quite
often a model or other controlled device has only four functions
to control. But the coder and decoder are relatively inexpensive
and are easy to wire up, so there is no harm in 'wasting' the

67

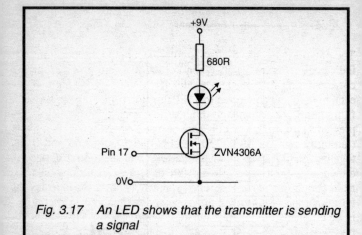

*Fig. 3.17   An LED shows that the transmitter is sending
a signal*

remaining 28 codes. Also, should you decide to extend the
system at a later date, it is only a matter of adding the extra key-
switches required and extending the circuitry of the receiver.
You do not need to reorganise the whole system.

To illustrate how to use this system we describe an example
based on the control of a motor boat. This is easily adaptable to
a wide range of other situations. We are aiming to provide as
many possible control functions while keeping the receiver and
driving circuit as simple as possible. The MV500 (and SL490)
have a 5-bit code word. That is to say, the code message consists of 5 bits which may each be high ('1') or low ('0'). Taken
together, they give the codes 00000, 00001, 00010, and so on to
11110, and finally 11111. This is a total of 32 codes, making it
possible to control up to 32 functions. However, if we do not
need as many functions as this, it is possible for the receiver circuit to be very simple indeed. At its simplest, we allocate one
function to each digit or bit. Each bit is used to toggle one function on or off. There are several ways of allocating functions to
output terminals, depending on exactly how you want the boat
to operate. For example, a system might have these 5 functions

A Motor on/off
B Forward/reverse

C Fast/slow
D Ahead/left
E Ahead/right

The control panel has 5 push-buttons, occupying the positions indicated in Figure 3.18 . When keys A to E are pressed, the corresponding line on the decoder ic (MV601) goes high. If each of these are connected to a J-K flip-flop (Fig. 3.1), the flip-flop output goes alternately high or low each time the key is pressed. This toggle action can be used to switch a motor (through a relay or MOSFET switch). Taking outputs A and B together, as in Figure 3.9 or Figure 3.10, we can control motor direction as well. Two speeds, fast or slow, can be obtained from output C by driving a relay which switches a series resistor into or out of the circuit that is powering the motor. Steering is accomplished by having a centrally-sprung rudder which is pulled to the left or right by a pair of solenoids driven (through relays or MOSFETs) by outputs D and E.

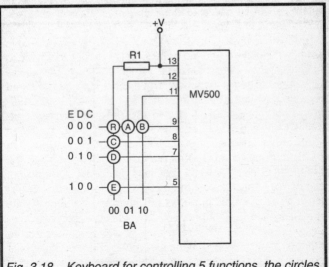

Fig. 3.18   Keyboard for controlling 5 functions, the circles
indicate push-buttons or keys

Figure 3.18 shows a sixth button (R) which produces an all-zero output from the decoder ic. This is not an essential part of the system but could be useful. An all-zero output is easily detected by connecting all 5 decoder output terminals to a 5-input NOR gate. In practice, use an 8-input NOR and wire some of its inputs to more than one of the decoder outputs. An all-zero output then produces a high output from the NOR gate. This can be used to drive another flip-flop for a sixth function but will automatically toggle off when any other function is selected. Another possible application is to connect the output of the NOR gate to the reset inputs of all flip-flops. Pressing R resets all functions to their initial state (motor off, forward drive, fast, straight ahead).

If further control functions such as 'sound the siren' or 'weigh anchor', or 'switch on navigation lights' are to be implemented, we need to expand the system by decoding the digits more fully. For example, a set of 8 functions can be implemented by using the keyboard arrangement shown in Figure 3.19. This operates on only three of the decoder outputs, which are decoded further by a 3-line to 8-line *decoder ic* (Fig. 3.20).

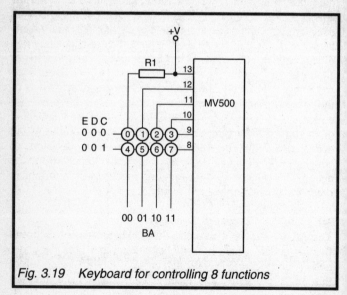

Fig. 3.19   Keyboard for controlling 8 functions

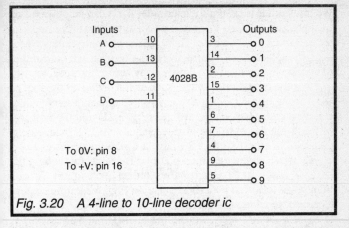

Fig. 3.20   A 4-line to 10-line decoder ic

We have used the word 'decoder' several times already but in this context we mean a special type of ic. Here, a decoder is a logic ic which has a number of outputs, each of which has a binary *address*. An output goes high when its address is put on the input lines of the ic. The 74HC137 and similar ics are available as 3-line to 8-line decoders but the 4028B 4-line to 10-line decoder (Fig. 3.20) is easier to use. For each of the binary numbers 0 to 9 (0000 to 1001) at the inputs, the corresponding one of the outputs goes high. If the inputs are 10 to 15 (1010 to 1111), all outputs are low. To use this as a 3-to-8 line decoder, we wire the A, B and C inputs to the corresponding outputs of the MV601 and the D input permanently to 0V. We use the eight outputs 0 to 7 of the 4028B. When one of the keys 0 to 7 of the transmitter is pressed, the corresponding output of the 4028B goes high. There are also 4-line to 16-line decoders, of which the 4514 and 4515 are examples. Outputs from the decoder ics may be used for toggling functions on or off, or in other ways, as described in Chapter 5.

MC145026 Coder and its Decoders

The MC145026, and also the SC41342, are easily-used and flexible coders which have the advantage that both the coder *and the* decoder may be operated on 4.5V to 15V. As a result of this, both transmitter and receiver can be run from batteries with a convenient range of voltages, and suitably small size. If the transmitter is used only intermittently, it can be powered by lithium coin cells, so making it possible to house the transmitter in a small key-fob case. These ics are primarily intended for security applications in which the signal from the transmitter has to be 'recognised' by the receiver before the receiver will allow some operation to occur, such as the opening of a door or the starting of a car. They also have applications in remote control. The coder has 9 address lines (Fig. 3.21) and the first five of these can be set to one of *three* states – '0', '1' or open circuit 'X'. In other words, they have a trinary input instead of a binary input. In the transmission, a '1' is sent as two long pulses, a '0' is sent as two short pulses and an open circuit 'X' as a long pulse followed by a short pulse. In Figure 3.21 the switches are set to address 001X1.

With 5 address lines, the number of different addresses is 3^5 or 243. This means that it is possible for a single control unit, which houses the coder, to control up to 243 different devices independently. But we would probably never require as many addresses as this provides. More often we may have only 2 or 3 controlled devices and quite often only 1. In this case, wiring the address pins is extremely simple. Although Figure 3.21 shows the address inputs each having 3-position switches (+V, open-circuit, 0V), Figure 3.22 shows a more practical situation in which pins 1 and 2 are permanently wired to 0V. This sets this particular controller to a single address in which the first two digits are zero and the remaining 3 are open-circuit (00XXX). Messages from this coder are accepted only by a decoder in which pins 1 and 2 are wired to 0V and the remainder are open-circuit. In whatever way we connect the address inputs, only a decoder with exactly matching connections will respond. The simplest possible address to set up is that for which all pins 1 to 5 are left unconnected (XXXXX). A decoder will respond only if all its pins 1 to 5 are likewise left unconnected.

As we shall see later, pins 6, 7, 9 and 10 may also be taken as address pins, so that a total of 3^9 (= 19683) addresses is available. However, address matching occurs before the second pulse of the ninth digit is received, so an 'X' is interpreted as a '1' and the number of recognisable addresses is reduced to $3^8 \times 2 = 13122$. Such a large number of addresses is advantageous

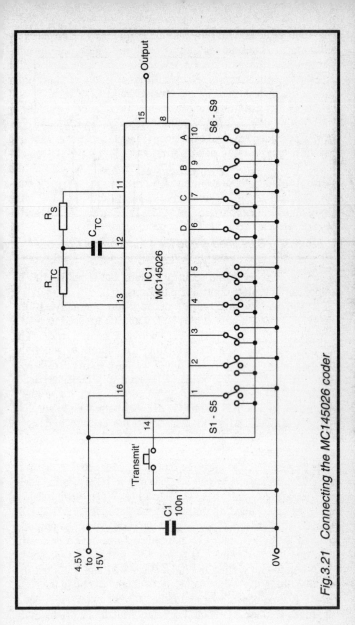

Fig.3.21 Connecting the MC145026 coder

73

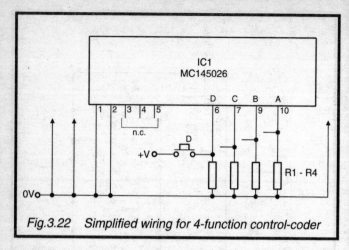

Fig.3.22   Simplified wiring for 4-function control-coder

when the ic is used in a security system, but is unlikely to be important in remote control applications.

If you use the MC145027 decoder (an alternative is the SC41343), the 4 inputs at pins 6, 7, 9 and 10 are used to send a 'message' (Fig. 3.23), in other words, a control code. The decoder has only 5 inputs for setting the address to which the decoder will respond. In the figure we have shown five 3-way switches set to 001X1, so as to respond to a coder set as in Figure 3.21. Once again, there is no need to cater for so many addresses. Figure 3.24 shows the decoder permanently wired to address 00XXX, so as to respond to the coder wired as in Figure 3.22. For the simplest address (XXXXX) leave all five pins unconnected.

In Figure 3.21 the message inputs are connected to *two*-way switches, because *data* can be sent only in binary form. There are 16 codes possible, from 0000 to 1111. When the message is sent, the corresponding outputs of the decoder (Fig. 3.23) are latched high or low, depending on the code. Since the output is latched the code remains on the four outputs until a new valid transmission is received. It is possible to have 4 switches or push-buttons for setting the input (Figs 3.21 and 3.22) but this entails setting the four switches individually to obtain the code, which is time-consuming and rather subject to errors. A better approach is to use a keyboard or rotary switch that produces the

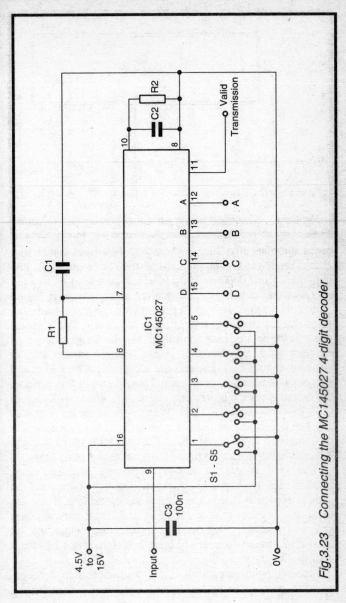

Fig.3.23 Connecting the MC145027 4-digit decoder

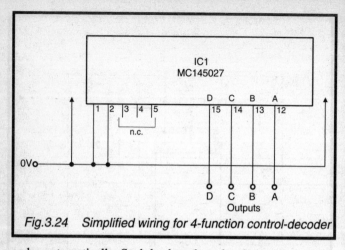

Fig.3.24   Simplified wiring for 4-function control-decoder

codes automatically. Such keyboards and switches can be purchased ready-made. The switches have 10 or 16 positions, giving codes from 0000 to 1001 (decimal switches) or to 1111
(hexadecimal switches). A keyboard may be built as in Figure
3.25. This is rather more work than buying one ready-made, but
gives you the chance to lay out the keys in a way that is appropriate to the device being controlled. This keyboard relies on an
encoder, an ic that has the reverse function to the decoder
shown in Figure 3.20. The encoder accepts input on 8 lines and
encodes this into data on 3 lines. Thus, if switch 6 is pressed,
the output gives the binary equivalent of 6, that is 110. Output
Q1 is low and outputs Q2 and Q4 are high. At the same time as
any key is pressed, output GS goes high. This is connected to
the 'transmit' input of the MC145026 so that a signal is transmitted whenever a key is pressed but not at any other time.

The 4532 encoder is actually a *priority encoder*, which
means that if two or more keys are pressed at the same time, the
code produced is that of the highest-numbered key. If you are
using this encoder to produce up to 8 different control codes
you will probably also need to connect the outputs of the
MC145027 to the decoder of Figure 3.20, to activate 1 of the 8
control outputs.

Another possible control unit is a joystick with 4 micro-
switches corresponding to forward, backward, left and right.

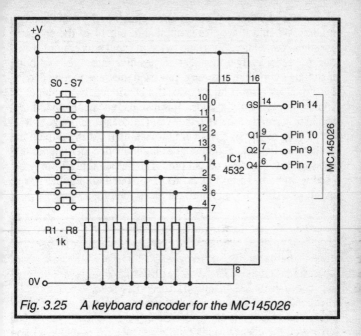

Fig. 3.25   A keyboard encoder for the MC145026

These give four codes 0001, 0010, 0100 and 1000. The corresponding four outputs of the decoder are used to produce the required actions. Some joysticks allow for diagonal movement, so that two switches are closed simultaneously. This gives a further set of codes, 0011, 0110, 1100 and 1001. These each cause two outputs of the decoder to go high, with two simultaneous actions (for example, move forward while turning left).

A much simpler arrangement is to have four push-buttons, as in Figure 3.22. Pressing *one button at a time* gives four codes, 0001, 0010, 0100, and 1000. This is sufficient for controlling four functions.

Finally, the inputs can be fed from CMOS logic, opening up many possibilities of logical remote control, including transmission of 4-bit analogue values.

The output from the coder may be sent to the decoder by direct wire connection, or by ultrasonic, IR, or 418MHz radio channels. The address switches (if any) on the decoder (Fig. 3.23) must be set to the same positions as in the coder, or the pins wired to 0V or +V, or left open-circuit in the same configuration. When a low pulse is applied to pin 14 of the coder, it transmits the address message twice in rapid succession. If the decoder receives two identical consecutive messages and both match its own address setting, its 'valid message received' output produces a short high pulse. If a continuously low input is applied to pin 14 of the coder, it transmits repeatedly and, if the signal is correctly received, the 'valid message' output goes low for as long as the signal is being transmitted. At the same time as the 'valid message' output goes high, the decoder latches the message bits on to the output pins. The output at pin 11 may be used to light an LED (Fig. 3.26) or to sound an audible warning device (Fig. 3.37) to indicate reception of a message.

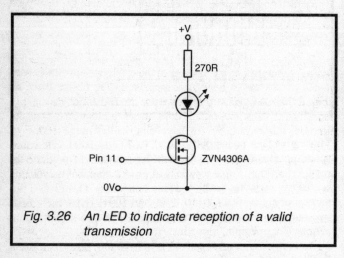

Fig. 3.26   An LED to indicate reception of a valid transmission

An alternative decoder is the MC145028, or SC41344. This differs from the MC145027 in that it has 9 inputs, all of which are trinary inputs, used for addressing. There is just a single output, the 'valid transmission' output of pin 11, which goes high when the address of the decoder matches the address of the coder. This could be used in a system in which there are several independent 'on–off' devices (or perhaps using toggling or multi-pulse coding). Each device has its own MC145028 set with its own address. All are under the control of a single

MC145026 controller with switchable addressing, so that any one of them may be brought under control as required.

For the tuning resistors in this system (R_{TC} in Figure 3.21; R1 and R2 in Figure 3.23) use 1% tolerance resistors. For the tuning capacitors (C_{TC} in Figure 3.21; C1 and C2 in Figure 3.23) use 1% close tolerance polystyrene capacitors. For the 100nF decoupling capacitors (C1 in Figure 3.21; C3 in Figure 3.23) use multilayer metallised polyester film capacitors.

Setting Up the MC145026 System

The coder and decoders include oscillators, which drive the signal-generating and signal-recognising circuits. These must operate at the same frequency f in both transmitter and receiver. So not only must the addresses be matching but the circuit must be set to the same frequency. The frequency of the coder is given by:

$$f = 1/2.3R_{TC}C_{TC}$$

In this equation, C_{TC} is the value of the capacitor plus the capacitance of the tracks between capacitor and ic (make these as short as possible) plus 12pF. If we use a capacitor of reasonably large value, for example 10nF, these corrections may be ignored. C_{TC} may be given any value in the range 100pF to 15µF. R_{TC} must be 10kΩ or over. Two convenient values are C_{TC} = 10nF, and R_{TC} 10kΩ. With these values, f = just over 4kHz. Then R_S takes a value about double that of R_{TC}. In this example, 22kΩ is suitable.

The capacitor and resistor values for the decoder are calculated from the values of C_{TC} and R_{TC}. For R_1 and C_1:

$$R_1C_1 = 3.95 \, R_{TC}C_{TC}$$

C_1 must be 400pF or more. In the example above:

$$R_1C_1 = 3.95 \times 10 \times 10^3 \times 10 \times 10^{-9} = 3.95 \times 10^{-4}$$

There are many possible pairs of values. An obvious choice is to make R_1 = 39kΩ. Then:

$$C_1 = (3.95 \times 10^{-4})/ (39 \times 10^3) = 1.013 \times 10^{-8} \approx 10 \times 10^{-9}$$

Use a 10nF capacitor for C_1.

For R_2 and C_2:
$$R_2C_2 = 77 \, R_{TC}C_{TC}$$

R_2 must be 100kΩ or more. C_2 must be 700pF or more. In the example above:

$$R_2C_2 = 77 \times 10 \times 10^3 \times 10 \times 10^{-9} = 7.7 \times 10^{-3}$$

If $C_2 = 22$nF, then:

$$R_2 = (7.7 \times 10^{-3}) / (22 \times 10^{-9}) = 350\text{k}\Omega$$

A 360kΩ is the closest standard value, or wire a 330kΩ resistor in series with a 18kΩ resistor.

The amount of current available from the outputs depends on the supply voltage. With a 5V supply, the outputs can supply up to 0.44mA. This is enough to supply a virtually unlimited number of CMOS logic inputs, or to operate a large number of MOSFET switches. With 10V supply the outputs supply up to 1.1mA, rising to 3.1mA with 15V supply.

Choosing a method
This chapter and the previous one have described a wide range of control methods. Which one is to be used in any given project? The choice will nearly always go to the simplest method that provides all the required control features and works reliably in the given conditions. When choosing a method, any possible expansion of the system in the future should be taken into account.

For any device that it simply to be triggered into action, or switched on for a short period, the single-pulse system is the obvious choice. A timing circuit within the controlled device (as in Fig. 5.6) can be used to give longer 'on' periods of fixed duration. If the device has to be switched on for longer periods of variable length and then switched off again, a two-stage sequential system provides the necessary toggle action.

If control of a few functions is required, and there is no objection to switching each on in turn briefly, the next simplest system is the multi-stage sequential system. Delays can be incorporated for those stages that must not be switched on unless required to operate.

For larger number of functions, and when stepping through them all is not acceptable, use a multiple-pulse system. The PPM ics (MV500, MV601 and SL490) allow up to 32 codes but are intended for use only with keyboards that connect sources to sinks. Also, the decoder must be operated on a regulated supply close to 5V. If you want to control two or more devices from a single transmitter you need to operate at two or more different frequencies. The MC145026/7 pair provide only 16 codes, but are very easy to use and both ics operate from batteries with a wide choice of supply voltages. Additionally they can use a wide range of input circuitry, including input from logic ics. Even if you intend to use only a few codes, it may be more economical to base your circuits on these ics. In particular, their error-checking features are invaluable in a noisy environment.

Projects

Below we describe some projects that make use of the sequential pulse and multiple-pulse systems described in this chapter. Although each project is aimed at a specific application, you will find it easy to adapt the projects to a very wide range of other applications. For explanations of the output/driving sections of the circuits you may need to look ahead to Chapter 5, where all the many output possibilities are described.

Project 6 – Remote Radio Set or Tape Recorder Control

This is an example of single-pulse control using ultrasound. In essence, it is a remotely controlled relay and can be used to switch on and off almost any battery-powered equipment. The transmitter is the unit described in Figure 2.1. The receiver is as described in Figure 2.2. Mount D2 on the front of the unit to give a visual indication that the signal has been received. The output of Figure 2.2 is taken to the toggle circuit of Figure 3.1. Without the toggle action, the radio is switched on only for as long as the transmit button is held down. With toggle action, the radio comes on when the button is briefly pressed and stays on until the button is pressed a second time. The output from

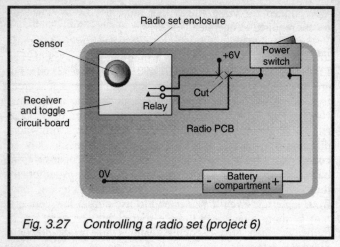

Fig. 3.27   Controlling a radio set (project 6)

Figure 3.1 is used to control a relay, which can be almost any normally-open type. Use either Figure 2.3 or 5.3 to switch the relay. The relay is wired in series with the instrument's own on-off switch. The simplest way to do this is to insert a 'battery sandwich' between two of the cells in the battery compartment (Fig. 2.15). Alternatively, cut the power lead to the radio as in Figure 3.27. It may be possible to accommodate the receiver and toggle circuit on a small circuit board for which space may be found inside the enclosure of the set. **Remember that, if the radio set is under warranty, cutting the lead may invalidate its guarantee.**

This project can be adapted to infra-red control using Figure 2.5 (transmitter), Figure 2.7 (receiver), and Figure 3.1 (toggle).

Project 7 – Radio Volume Control

This could also be used as a DC motor speed control or lamp brightness control. The transmitter and receiver are as described in previous projects, either ultrasonic or infra-red. The output from the receiver goes to the circuit of Figure 3.5, which goes through 4 stages as the transmit button is pressed repeatedly. The output of this circuit is decoded as in Figure 3.8. The four outputs each go high in turn. These outputs are used to drive four relays, each through a MOSFET. Thus each output from Figure 3.8 switches a relay as shown in Figure 2.3 or 5.3. If reed relays are used, the CMOS outputs can generally drive these directly. The relays are connected to resistors which are

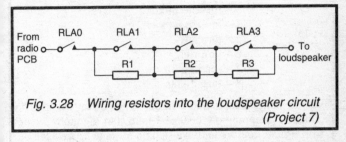

Fig. 3.28   Wiring resistors into the loudspeaker circuit (Project 7)

wired in series with the loudspeaker (Fig. 3.28). They have normally-closed (NC contacts), or you can use the NC sides of relays with changeover contacts. The switching has four stages. With RLA0 energised, the sound is turned off. With RLA1, 2 or 3 energised, resistors R1, R2 or R3 are in turn put in series with the loudspeaker. The exact values required for the resistors must be found by trial. As a starting point, assuming an 8Ω loudspeaker, try R1 = 22Ω, R2 = 47Ω and R3 = 100Ω. Use 0.25W or 0.5W resistors, possibly resistors of higher wattage if your speaker is rated higher.

Project 8 – Model Vehicle Control

This project provides a wide range of controls, but operates on a single pulse system. The transmitter is one of the standard ultrasonic, infra-red or cable single-pulse circuits. You could use the simple radio control system of Project 5 but preferably use a coded system as discussed in Project 12. The receiver is also one of the standard types. The receiver output is used to step on the Johnson counter of Figure 3.12, which in this project is set for a 9-stage cycle by connecting output 8 pin 9 to IC2. This project illustrates some new ways of using decoder outputs and its principles are applicable to a wide range of controlled devices, including boats, planes, radio sets and many others.

Let us suppose that the required actions are:

0 – do nothing
1 – start motor
2 – stop motor
3 – forward motor
4 – reverse motor
5 – turn left
6 – turn right
7 – sound horn
8 – flash lights

There are some complications in this scheme that we have not met before. Stepping on to stage 1 is to start the motor, which is to *continue running* until we step on to stage 2. We need one stage to start the motor and another stage to stop it. This calls for a set-reset flip-flop to control the motor. However, if we are at stage 1 and want the motor to continue running while we sound the horn (stage 7), there is the problem that the motor will stop as soon as we step to stage 2. Even if we step through quickly, it is likely that the flip-flop will be triggered and the motor will stop. The key to this problem is to insert delays in the system so that, provided we do not linger unduly on stage 1 or 2, we are able to step through these stages without changing the state of the motor. The circuit in Figure 3.29 has low-pass filters in series between the outputs from the decoder and the inputs to the flip-flop. They delay the action by about 0.3s, giving time to step through the stage. Either of the motor control circuits of Figures 3.9 or 3.10 may be used for controlling motor stop/start (A inputs).

The circuit for making the motor run in forward or reverse directions are exactly as in Figure 3.29, connected to the B inputs of Figures 3.9 or 3.10. The way that turning left and right is implemented depends on the steering mechanism of the vehicle. Possibly two solenoids could be used, one to pull the mechanism to the left, the other to pull it to the right. Solenoids are switched by circuits such as Figures 2.3 (omitting D2) or 5.3.

We will assume that the simplest solution is adopted for sounding the horn (or other audio device), that is to say it

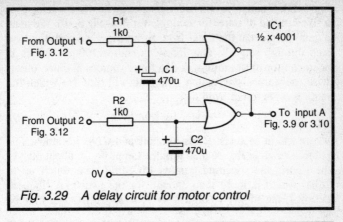

Fig. 3.29   A delay circuit for motor control

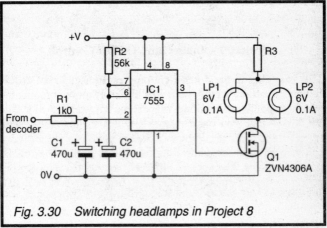

Fig. 3.30   Switching headlamps in Project 8

sounds for as long as the circuit is in stage 7. The horn can be driven by a simple transistor switch. Ideally there would be a delay on the input side of this to prevent the horn from bleeping as we pass quickly through stage 7, but this is hardly necessary.

There are several options for lamp control. We could simply turn them on for as long as the circuit is in stage 8; use a transistor switch, a delay is not essential. Another option is to use two outputs to control the lamps (lamps on and lamps off, using

85

Fig 3.29). Finally, we can use a timer to switch on the lamps for a fixed period of time, for example for 30s (Fig 3.30). We need a delay to prevent the timer from being triggered each time we step through stage 8. The 7555 can source 100mA, which is adequate for most models. A 555 timer sources 200mA, otherwise use a transistor switch. The length of time for which the lamp is on is found from:

$$t = 1.1 \times R2C2$$

where t is in seconds, R2 is in ohms and C2 is in farads. The values shown in Figure 3.30 turn the lamps on for about 30s. In the figure, the specified type of MOSFET can switch up to 1.3A, which is more than enough for the two 0.1A filament lamps. If the supply voltage is 9V or more, resistor R3 may be required.

Project 9 – Table Lamp On/Off Control

This is similar to the porch-light project (Project 3) but differs in two important ways. The mains circuit is more complicated and is capable of handling bigger currents (Fig. 3.31). The TIC225M triac can pass up to 8A which means that several mains-voltage lamps can be switched in parallel and the circuit can also be used for controlling an electric heater or a mains-powered motor. The second difference is that this is a toggle-action control: a pulse turns the lamp on for as short or long a time as you wish until a second pulse turns it off. Because the mains circuit is more complicated, be sure to **read the AC mains precautions** at the beginning of the book before you start construction.

The circuit is suitable for all types of control, though probably ultra-sound or IR will be favoured. As it is likely to be operated at relatively short range – the main purpose of the system is to control a table or standard lamp from a nearby armchair – the simplest of the transmitters and receivers are adequate. The output from the receiver goes to a J-K flip-flop (as in Fig. 3.1). When output Q is high, MOSFET Q1 is turned on, current flows through the low-voltage side of the MOC3020 opto-coupler, the opto-triac conducts and the power triac conducts.

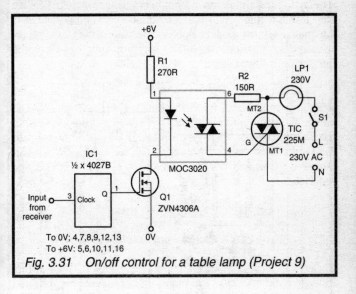

Fig. 3.31   On/off control for a table lamp (Project 9)

Project 10 — Ultrasonically-controlled Switch for Mains-powered Devices

Figure 3.32 is a general-purpose circuit for controlling devices that operate on relatively high voltage or with alternating current. Other receiver circuits could replace the ultrasonic receiver of Figure 2.2.

Project 11 – Mobile Panic Button

This project makes use of the fact that remote control allows us to control a device from almost anywhere in a room or building (with a radio system), and without the need for trailing wires connecting the control unit to the controlled device. Originally the project was seen as a way of providing a handy and portable panic button that an invalid or elderly person could carry

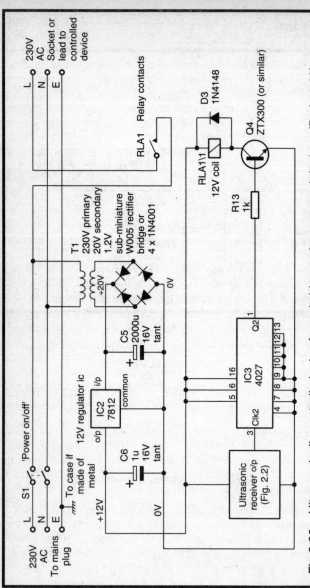

Fig.3.32 Ultra-sonically controlled relay for switching mains-powered devices (Project 10)

88

around on their person, yet could trigger a really loud alarm sound from a centrally-placed installation. Subsequently, other applications suggested themselves, including a sensory device for the security system which could be inconspicuous and not need connecting wires. Connecting wires are often a problem in a security system. For one thing they are usually unsightly and may be impossible to conceal. A second point is that, if they are visible, they give information to the intruder who may then be able to circumvent the system.

The system is based on the MC145026 ic described earlier in this chapter. It might be thought a waste of the enormous addressing capacity of this system to use only one of its addresses, but the uniqueness of the signalling codes means that the alarm is very unlikely to be triggered accidentally by other systems being operated in the same room. Figure 3.33 shows the transmitter to be carried by the user. In a radio system, the output of IC1 is connected directly to pin 5 of the transmitter module. The quiescent current of the circuit is no more than 0.3μA, so a PP3 9V battery will last a very long time. The input to the ic is a push-button, acting here as a panic button. This should be mounted on the case so that it can not be pressed accidentally. The output of the ic drives a pair of infra-red LEDs or a 418MHz transmitter. Values of R_{TC}, R_S and C_{TC} may be as shown in Figure 3.33. We have not shown any addressing connections because, if only one system is in use, it can have address 00000. Simply leave all the address pins unconnected. Similarly, there is no message either; the fact that the ic is transmitting a 0000 message is sufficient.

The receiver in Figure 3.34 is equally simple to construct. We do not use the address outputs but simply take the 'valid transmission received' out (pin 11) to drive the audible warning device. This can be one of the very loud solid-state warblers or sirens. Rated at over 100dB, most of them require only a few tens of milliamps. The circuit in Figure 3.34 sounds the alarm for as long as the panic button is pressed and held down. Using one of the circuits of Chapter 5 it is not difficult to adapt the circuit so that the alarm sounds continuously for a longer period after the button has been released.

The circuits can be adapted in very many ways. Instead of a push-button, there could be a normally-open micro-switch

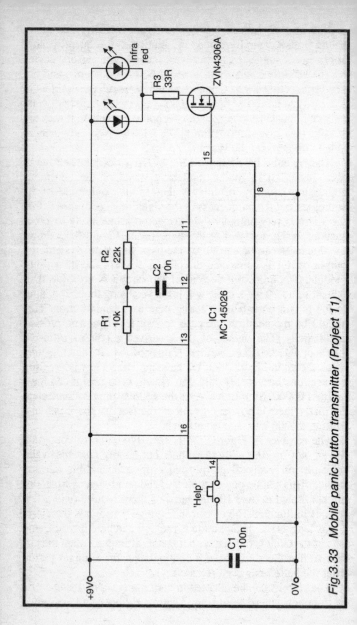

Fig.3.33 Mobile panic button transmitter (Project 11)

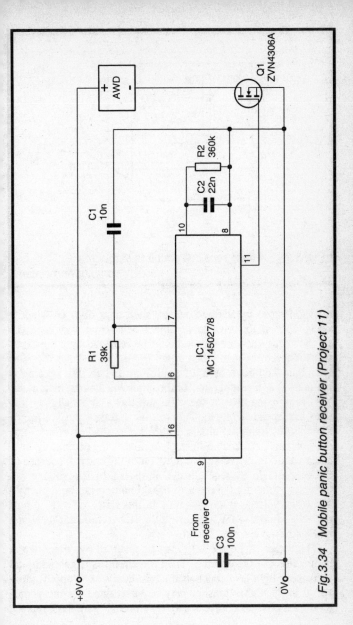

Fig.3.34 Mobile panic button receiver (Project 11)

91

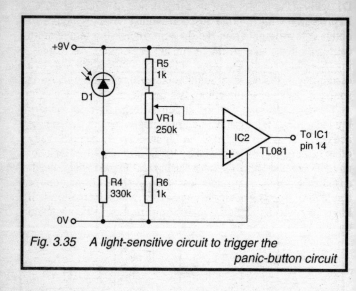

Fig. 3.35   A light-sensitive circuit to trigger the
panic-button circuit

made to close by various events, such as a door or window
being opened, or a valuable object being removed from the
sideboard top. Or the button could be replaced by a pressure-
mat hidden underneath the carpet. Figure 3.35 shows a circuit
to trigger the circuit by a light-sensitive switch. The op amp is
being used as a comparator. In the quiescent state of the circuit,
VR1 is adjusted to make the voltage at the (−) input slightly less
than that at the (+) input. This results in the output voltage of
the op amp swinging almost to 9V. If the shadow of an intruder falls on D1 (a visible-light photodiode), the decreasing light
causes a fall in the voltage at junction of D1 and R4, because of
the decrease in leakage current through D1. The voltage fall
causes a fall at the (+) input of the op amp, bringing it slightly
below the voltage at the (−) input. In this state, the op amp output falls almost to 0V, triggering the IC1 to transmit its signal
and cause the alarm to sound.

The action of Figure 3.35 may be reversed by reversing the
connections to the op amp. Then the circuit is triggered by an
increasing light level, such as the headlamps of an approaching
car at night. Other sensors may be substituted for the photodiode. An obvious choice is a thermistor. In Figure 3.35, replace

D1 with a thermistor having a resistance of 47kΩ at 25°C. Replace R4 with a 47kΩ resistor. Adjust VR1, as before to obtain a low output from the op amp. Increasing temperature causes the resistance of the thermistor to decrease, so increasing the voltage at the (+) input. When the temperature rises to a certain level, the op amp output swings high and the alarm is sounded. This has applications as a fire alarm.

We have assumed that the circuit is to be used to sound a loud alarm, but this is only one of the many devices that can be activated. Instead of the AWD in Figure 3.34 we can place any other device that can be driven by 9V DC. Possibilities include: an LED (with series resistor), a flashing LED (no resistor needed), a filament lamp, a rather less strident sounder, a motor, or a solenoid. Another possibility is a relay, which then allows all kinds of devices, including mains-power units, to be switched on remotely.

Project 12 – Message Pager

This is an extension of Project 11, having the facility to convey up to 8 prearranged messages. The transmitter sends one of 8 codes and, on reception of the coded message a numeric display on the receiver shows a number in the range 0 to 7. Each number corresponds with a message according to a list of messages previously agreed upon. Like the previous project, this system also makes use of the MC154026/7 coder and decoder so that only one receiver responds to the message. In Figure 3.36 the keyboard and encoder of Figure 3.25 are shown providing a 3-bit input to the coder. The fourth bit is used to enable the coder. It goes high when any of the keys is pressed, causing the coder to send its code word (twice, or many times if the key is held depressed). No connections are shown for the address inputs. They can be left open as shown or connected in various combinations to +V and 0V to produce a unique address, which must be matched by the address wired into the receiver circuit. Values of R_{TC}, R_S and C_{TC} may be as shown in Figure 3.21. As in the previous projects the circuit is best mounted in a small hand-held remote-control enclosure with either an internal helical antenna, or with a whip antenna projecting from the

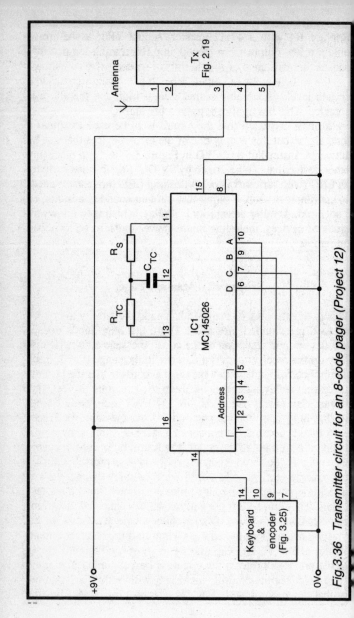

Fig. 3.36 Transmitter circuit for an 8-code pager (Project 12)

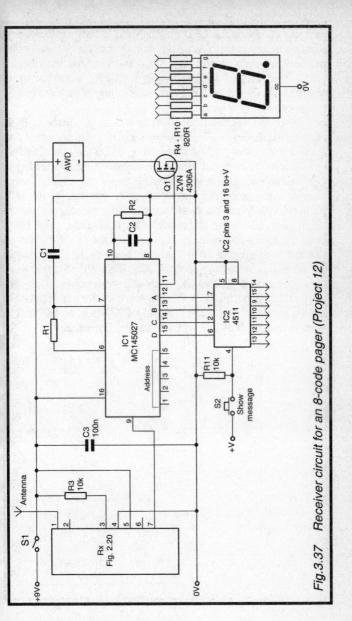

Fig.3.37 Receiver circuit for an 8-code pager (Project 12)

95

case. As an option, an LED may be used to indicate that transmission is occurring. You could actually use the decimal point of the 7-segment display as a valid transmission indicator, if you prefer. This is switched by a MOSFET transistor as in Figure 5.1b, the input to the transistor being taken from pin 14 of the encoder.

The coded output from IC1 is fed to a binary-to-BCD decoder (IC2, Fig. 3.37). This produces the signals needed to drive a 7-segment LED display. Note that a common-*cathode* type display is essential. Since the receiver unit is intended to be small and portable it is not feasible to provide a battery large enough to power the display continuously. Instead, the BLANK input of IC2 (pin 4) is held low, blanking the display except when push-button S2 is pressed. On hearing the brief bleep from the AWD, the recipient presses S2, lighting the display so that the code number (0 to 7) can be read. In the diagram, pin 15 of IC1 is wired to pin 6 of IC2. This allows for a 4-bit message, so that digits 8 and 9 can also be received. This connection works correctly in this project, even though it has only a 3-bit message. If preferred pin 15 of IC1 may be left unconnected, and pin 6 of IC2 wired to the 0V line instead.

Chapter 4

STRATEGIES

Chapters 2 and 3 have described the main ways of generating a remote control signal and making it produce the required action in the controlled device. In this chapter we look at techniques used to widen the scope of remote control from on/off switching to dealing with analogue quantities, using computers and microcontrollers, voice control, and an introduction to control with feedback.

Analogue Techniques

Most of the signals we use in remote control are *binary* signals, represented as 0's and 1's or 'lows' and 'highs'. They are used to control binary operations, such as stop/run, left/right, lamp on/off. The signals are delivered as a series of pulses. It is sometimes necessary for a signal to represent an *analogue* quantity. This is a quantity that it capable of taking any value over a given range. Analogue quantities include time, temperature, speed, and angle. Such quantities are represented in a signal by an electrical analogue, often a voltage. For example, we may represent an angle by a voltage by using a joystick, as in Figure 4.1. The position of the joystick is represented by another analogue quantity, the resistance between the two wired terminals of the potentiometer. This is connected to a circuit in which changes in the resistance are converted to changes in a voltage. Alternatively, we may connect the ends of the track to +V and 0V; then the voltage at the wiper varies with the position of the joystick.

It is possible to transmit an analogue signal in the same way as a varying voltage or current. With a wired direct connection, this is easy since the varying current is sent along a wire directly to the controlled device. There it drives a motor, for example at a proportional speed. This kind of signal could also be used in an optical fibre system, with the brightness of the light being an analogue of joystick position. But direct transmission of the analogue does not work well with ultrasound or radiated IR, for the strength of the received signal depends on the

97

distance from the transmitter. There are also unknown factors inherent in the transmitting device and in the amount of amplification at the receiver. Transmitting an analogue quantity as an analogue signal is basically a very unreliable technique.

The solution to this problem is to transmit the data as pulses. Pulses are all of the same amplitude but vary in one of three different ways:

1 Proportional control: transmit pulses at regular intervals but make the length of the pulse proportional to the analogue quantity. This technique is used in controlling servos, as described later in this chapter. The main limitation is that noise may introduce errors into the determination of pulse length by the receiver. Feedback can overcome this problem. For example, when applying proportional control to a model aeroplane, the operator can watch the behaviour of the model and adjust the controls to compensate for errors. Servo-control is described in Chapter 5, and a simpler pulse-length technique is described below.

2 Pulse frequency control: make the frequency of the pulses proportional to the analogue quantity. The circuits are simple, since there are ics designed for converting voltage to frequency and frequency to voltage. Usually it is easy to detect a transmission of regular frequency against a background of noise, so this technique is good for noisy environments.

3 Coding: the numerical value is converted into digital form and transmitted as a sequence of '1's (pulse) '0's (no pulse). Generally we use a special analogue-to-digital converter ic to generate the code. At the receiving end the code is re-converted to a voltage, using a digital-to-analogue ic.

Pulse-length Control

This technique is specially intended for controlling the speed of a low-voltage motor, which is perhaps the most frequent objective of remote control of models. The control is provided in the transmitter (Fig. 4.2), which generates pulses of variable length. Instead of controlling speed by varying the strength of current supplied to the motor, we always supply the full current,

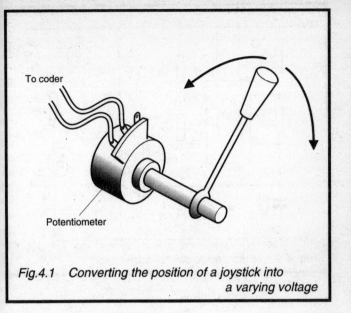

Fig.4.1   Converting the position of a joystick into a varying voltage

but vary the lengths of time for which it is on or off. This method is ideal for use in single-pulse systems and can be used also for lamp brightness control.

The 7555 timer in Figure 4.2 is wired as an astable multivibrator with a frequency of about 18kHz. The exact frequency does not matter, but it is high enough to ensure that the motor does not run jerkily. Instead of taking the output from pin 3 of the timer, we take it from the positive side of the capacitor. As the timer operates, the voltage across the capacitor ramps up from $V/3$ to $2V/3$, where V is the supply voltage. In the figure we have made V equal to 6 volts, so the output ramps up from 2V to 4V, dropping sharply and repeating to produce a sawtooth signal (Fig. 4.3). This fed to an op amp, and we use one with FET inputs so that it draws almost no current and does not upset the action of the timer. The op amp is wired as a comparator; this particular op amp having a high slew rate so that it follows input changes rapidly.

The other input comes from the wiper of a variable resistor. This may be simply a potentiometer with a knob, or a slider

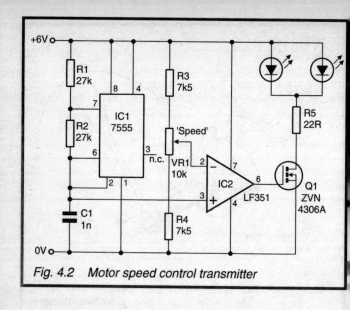

Fig. 4.2   Motor speed control transmitter

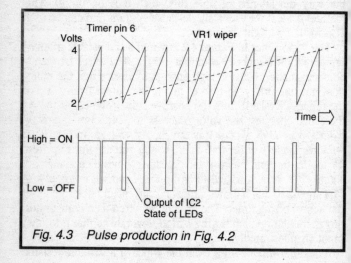

Fig. 4.3   Pulse production in Fig. 4.2

potentiometer or a 'joystick' made up as in Figure 4.1 but with connections to all three terminals.. If the potentiometer is attached to a part of a machine (such as an arm of a robot) the output is a measure of the position of the arm. On the other hand if we are simply trying to control an analogue quantity such as the speed of a motor, all we need is an ordinary control knob which we turn one way or the other to adjust the speed. Or we can use a slider potentiometer. As suggested earlier, the ends of the track are usually connected to 0V and +V, with the control voltage being taken from the wiper. This is adequate for most purposes, especially when we can observe the controlled device and check that it is responding as required.

The resistors in series with the potentiometer have values which bring its track ends to slightly below 2V at the lower end and slightly above 4V at the upper end. We can obtain any voltage in the range 2V to 4V by turning VR1. If VR1 is set to give slightly less than 2V, the voltage from the timer is always greater than this, so the output of the op amp is always high. This turns on the MOSFET continuously, and so the LEDs are on continuously, producing one long pulse which keeps the motor running at full speed. If VR1 is set to give slightly more than 4V, the voltage from the timer is never as high as this. The MOSFET, LEDs and motor are continuously off. At intermediate voltages the output of the op amp is high for part of the time (Fig. 4.3). It gives a square wave with fixed frequency (18kHz) but variable mark-space ratio, which determines the speed of the motor.

A suitable receiver is Figure 2.7, with its output fed to a MOSFET which controls the motor current. A suitable switching circuit is Figure 5.3. The advantage of this system, quite apart from its simplicity, is that it gives fine control over motor speed. It is particularly good when a motor has to be run slowly and with a varying load. When we control a motor by varying the strength of current, it is easy for the motor to stall when the current is small. In this system the motor receives full-strength current pulses, even if they are short ones, and these keep the motor turning.

Pulse Frequency Control

As in the method described in the previous section, an analogue quantity (voltage) is transmitted as a train of pulses of fixed amplitude. Instead of varying the length of the pulses, we vary their frequency. The circuit in Figure 4:4 produces a square-wave signal, the frequency of which is proportional to the voltage at the wiper of the variable resistor. The CMOS 4046 ic is really a complete phase locked loop system. The ic includes a voltage-controlled oscillator, which can be used on its own. Power supply can be in the range +3V to +15V. When the analogue input is half the supply voltage and if R2 is omitted, the central frequency f_0 is:

$$f_0 = \frac{1}{R1 \times C}$$

This applies when the supply voltage is 15V, but f_0 is slightly lower at lower supply voltages. R1 must be between 10kΩ and 1MΩ. C1 must be greater than 50pF; add 32pF to the value of C1 to allow for input capacitance. As the analogue input sweeps from 0V to the supply voltage, the frequency sweeps from 0Hz to $2f_0$. The relationship is not exactly linear, especially when the input is less than 2V, but is reasonably linear over the remainder of the range and certainly good enough for many remote control applications.

The frequency range may be offset from 0Hz by including R2. The calculations are somewhat complicated and the relationships are not linear. The simplest approach is to try the effects of various values of R2, making R2 about one fifth of R1 as a starting-point. The value of R3 depends on supply voltage; 22Ω is a suitable value if the supply voltage is 6V. This gives a current of just under 100mA through each LED.

Project 13 at the end of this chapter illustrates how to use this VCO and the frequency-to-voltage circuit described in the next paragraph.

A signal of varying frequency received from the transmitter of Figure 4.4 may be re-converted to a varying voltage by the circuit of Figure 4.5. The circuit requires only a few milliamps so is suitable for battery-powered equipment. The input comes from the receiver circuit. The output goes to the controlled

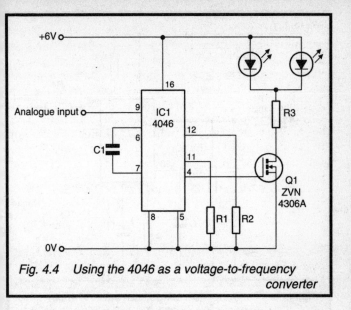

Fig. 4.4   Using the 4046 as a voltage-to-frequency
converter

device, but note that the maximum output is less than the supply voltage. For example if the supply is 9V the maximum output is about 5V. The conversion of voltage to frequency and of frequency to voltage depends upon many factors. The best place to determine the relationships is on the workbench.

Analogue Output Control
Often we want to control an analogue quantity, such as the volume of sound or the brightness of a lamp, using a single-pulse or sequential pulse system. Here we are not transmitting the analogue as such, as in the two systems described above. Rather, we transmit a digital signal which generates the analogue in the receiver. In Figure 4.6 a 4-stage counter receives a pulsed input which originally comes from a single-pulse transmitter. You can use ultrasound (Figs 2.1 and 2.2), infra-red (Figs 2.5 and 2.7) or a cable connection from a debounced push-button (Fig. 3.3).

As each pulse arrives, the counter is incremented by one step. Its outputs run through the binary sequence from 0000 to 1111 and then repeat, indefinitely. The op amp summer circuit

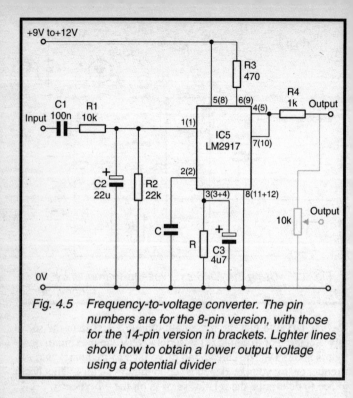

Fig. 4.5   *Frequency-to-voltage converter. The pin
numbers are for the 8-pin version, with those
for the 14-pin version in brackets. Lighter lines
show how to obtain a lower output voltage
using a potential divider*

with weighted resistors is a basic digital-to-analogue converter. As the counter output increases from 0000 to 1111, the
output voltage increases from 0V to a specified maximum voltage in 15 equal steps. When it is at the maximum, the next pulse
takes it to zero, from where in increases again with successive
pulses.

This system can be adapted to a 3-stage counter, giving an 8-
stage cycle, or even to a 2-stage counter. In the latter case we
might use two connected flip-flops (Fig. 3.5) as the counter. It
could also be adapted to more stages.

Looking at the circuit in more detail, the Schmitt input
NAND gate (IC1) is used to sharpen the output from the receiving circuit. If reception conditions are good, you may find that
this is not necessary. As a pulse is received, the input to the gate

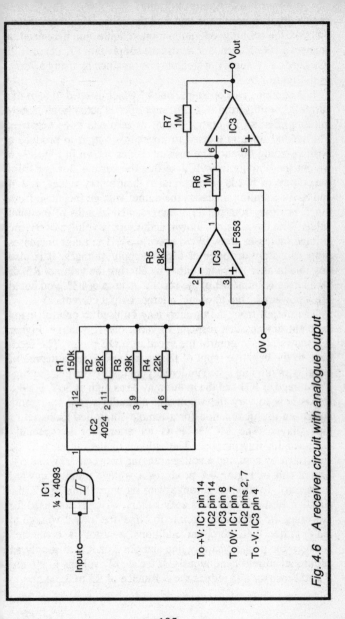

Fig. 4.6 A receiver circuit with analogue output

goes high, its output goes low, and the counter is incremented. To make the counting operation more reliable, you may need to connect a 100nF capacitor across the supply pins (7, 14) of IC2. IC3 needs a -V supply, which may be obtained by using a 7660, as in Figure 2.9.

IC3 contains two op amps, one of which is used to sum the currents coming from IC2. The amplifier is actually an inverting amplifier, so its output begins at zero and goes negative. The second op amp is used to invert this output to produce a positive-going output. The resistor values shown in Figure 4.6 weight the outputs from IC2 so that the current flowing from the outputs of IC2 is proportional to their binary values, 1, 2, 4 and 8. As counting proceeds the output voltage (negative from pin 1, positive from pin 7) is incremented in $\frac{1}{16}$ths of the total value. With the resistors shown, and a supply voltage of 6V the voltage increases from 0V to about 4.5V. The range increases proportionately at lower or higher supply voltages. It is also possible to alter the range either by altering the value of R5, or by altering R7. Instead of the second op amp of IC3, you could use a power op amp to obtain a larger output current.

The output from the op amp may be used to control many different devices that respond to variations in voltage. Figure 4.7 shows how to control the speed of a DC motor. The feedback to the negative input of the op amp provides a degree of stability in running speed under varying load. Note that the supply voltage of IC4 and the motor may be as high as 36V. Fig 4.8 shows how to vary the volume of an audio signal by remote control, a useful function for a remote-controlled radio set or tape player. The MC3340P is an attenuator ic specially designed for this purpose. The volume of the output may be controlled by applying a voltage ranging between 3.5V and 6V. The circuit of Figure 4.6 produces a voltage ranging upward from zero. To produce a range with its upper limit at 6V, the circuit is best powered from a 9V battery, which is also used for powering the attenuator circuit. To offset the lowest voltage to 3.5V rather than zero, an additional resistor is connected between the positive supply line and pin 2 of IC3 to supply an additional current continuously. If the supply voltage is 9V, use a 10kΩ resistor and reduce the resistance of R5 to 3.3kΩ.

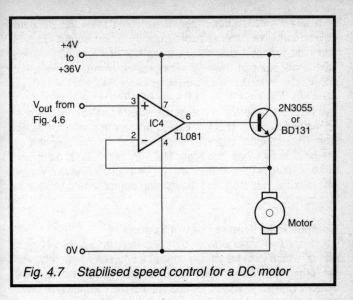

Fig. 4.7   Stabilised speed control for a DC motor

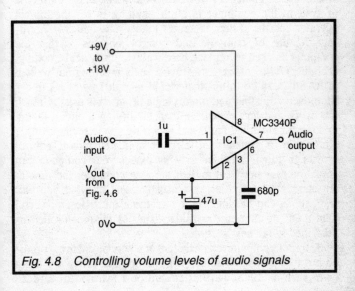

Fig. 4.8   Controlling volume levels of audio signals

Resistor values quoted above are taken from the standard ranges and give only an approximately linear output. This is adequate for most purposes, particularly since resistors often have a tolerance of only 5%. For greater linearity and a more accurately defined range, use 1% resistors. Make R1 = 160kΩ, R2 = 80kΩ, R3 = 40kΩ and R4 = 20kΩ. You many need to wire two resistors in series to obtain the required values, or use pre-set potentiometers. If R5 = 10kΩ, this would produce a range from 0V to the full supply voltage, but the op amp output may not be able to swing that high. If R5 is, say, 8.2kΩ, the maximum voltage is 0.82 of the supply. For example with a 6V supply, maximum is 4.6V and the op amp output should be able to rise to this.

Computers in Remote Control Systems

There are two aspects to using computers in control systems, one of which is to be able to control a computer remotely, and the other of which is for the computer to control external devices remotely. Some systems control the computer, in other systems the computer takes control and, in a third type, of system the computer is involved in both ways. In the third type of system, the computer is often standing in for the human operator and the system is almost totally automatic. A significant feature of computerised control systems is that the computer is used to replace hardware (logic systems, coding, decoding) with software. Software, such as a program written in BASIC, can do things that would take dozens of ics to do. Moreover, adjusting and modifying a program is usually much less work and less expensive than modifying a circuit-board, looking for electrical faults and re-wiring whole sections of the circuit. So, if you have a fairly complicated remote control project in mind, consider to what extent your computer can help. You may not want to dedicate your computer full-time to remote-control activities, and usually most of what you will want to do can be done with something much less powerful than a PC. In that case consider using as microcontroller, as described in the next section.

Before a computer can exercise any sort of control, it must be put into contact with the world around it. Often we use a *card*, such as the SoundBlaster card or a fax/modem card, to make the connection. We could build a card for interfacing the computer to a remote control system, but this is a fairly complicated task, mainly because we have to include all the addressing circuitry which allows the computer to find where the card resides in its memory map. A simpler system is to let the remote control system reside at one of the existing memory ports, the printer port. This means that it is not possible to use the printer at the same time as the remote control system is running, but this is usually no disadvantage. It makes it easier to switch from using the printer to running the control system and back again quickly if we use a *switch box*. This is a ready-made unit (though not too difficult to make at home) which is connected by cable to the printer socket on the rear of the computer. The box has a 2- or 3-position rotary switch and two or three 25-pin sockets like the printer port socket. The printer is plugged into one of these sockets and the remote control interface is plugged into one of the others.

In the IBM PCs, the printer interface is generally referred to as LPT1. This port comprises three groups of input and output lines. Each group has an address, which specifies its location in the memory map. Most handbooks state that the three groups, or *registers* of LPT1 are located at addresses 0378, 0379 and 037A, all addresses being expressed as hexadecimal numbers. But you may find that your computer is different. In some models the addresses are 0278, 0279, and 027A instead. Further, in the author's IBM computer the addresses are 03BC, 03BD and 03BE. The first step is to find the addresses in your own computer. Maybe they are given in the handbook but, more likely, you will need to run the configuration program. The IBM configuration utility is run by pressing the F1 key while the computer is counting its memory (almost immediately after it has been switched on. The information is displayed in 4 pages or screens. The address of the printer port is given under 'System Setup' on page 2. Here, under the entry 'Parallel Port' we find [Parallel_1 (3BC-IRQ7)]. The '3BC' or whatever other number may be listed here is the first address in the block of memory allocated to the parallel port, otherwise referred to as LPT1. It is possible that other addresses may have been allocated to this port in other models of the IBM-PC or in versions from other manufacturers. In all the descriptions which follow we shall

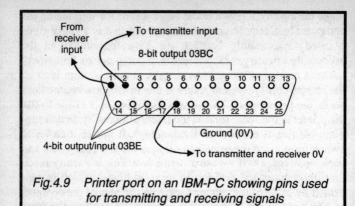

*Fig.4.9   Printer port on an IBM-PC showing pins used
for transmitting and receiving signals*

refer to the addresses used in our model (6381) of the IBM-PC.

Connection to the printer port is made with a micro-minia-
ture D-type 25-pin plug. You may be able to buy this with the
wires already soldered to the pins, or to buy a standard printer
lead and cut off the plug that goes into the socket on the printer. For simple applications only a few of the pins need connections, in which case it is best to buy a bare plug and solder in
the wires as you need them. Fig 4.9 shows the layout at the
printer port, the pins being viewed as seen when you stand
looking at the sockets from behind the computer. Of the three
registers we use only 2 in this chapter. They are allocated to the
pins as follows:

Address	Pin	Data bit	Function
03BC	2	0	8-bit output register: bit 0 is the least
	3	1	significant bit, bit 7 is the most
	4	2	significant bit. This register can also
	5	3	be read from as a check that the bits
	6	4	have been correctly set.
	7	5	
	8	6	
	9	7	

110

03BE	1	0	4-bit input/output register, which we
	14	1	use only for input; bits 4–7 not used.
	16	2	Bit 2 is read and written to normal-
	17	3	ly; bits 0, 1, and 3 are inverted.

Pins 18-25 are connected to the computer ground (0V) line. Any circuit connected directly to the computer must have its 0V line connected to one of these pins. The structure of the registers at 03BD and 03BE is a little complicated but the ways around this are explained below. For further details of the registers, see BP 377, Practical Electronic Control Projects.

The Computer as a Remote Controller

The easiest output device is one or more IR LEDs. The interface in Figure 4.10 also has a visible light LED which flashes at the same time as the IR LEDs to make it easier to check that the interface and program are working properly. It is powered either with a +5V regulated power supply or a 6V *battery*. The 6V line must not be connected directly to the computer or printer port. The values of R1 and R2 depend on the types of

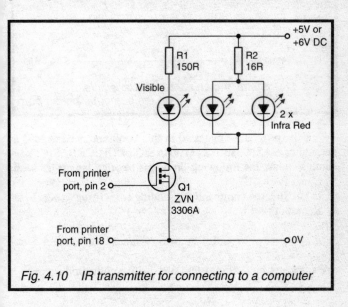

Fig. 4.10   IR transmitter for connecting to a computer

111

LEDs used and the number of IR LEDs run in parallel. The LED is controlled through bit 0 of the 03BC register. All that is needed is a wire from that bit (pin 2 of the connector) and one from the ground (0V), which may be any one of pins 18–25. The battery power supply of the transmitter is independent of the computer's power supply and **no direct connection must be made between the power supply line and any of the pins of LPT1, or any part of the computer or its peripherals.** When connecting this and other projects to the computer, **double-check all connections** before switching on the project. Failure to do this may result in damage to the ics of the computer port. Alternatively, the computer may be used to switch the ultrasonic transmitter of Figure 2.1. Omit S1, R1 and the connection to the supply and wire pin 2 of the port socket directly to pin 1 of IC1, as in Figure 4.11. **Run the transmitter on a 6V battery.**

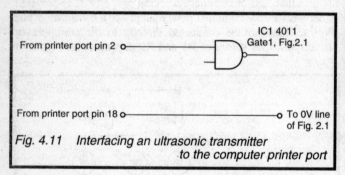

IC1 4011
Gate1, Fig.2.1

From printer port pin 2

From printer port pin 18

To 0V line
of Fig. 2.1

*Fig. 4.11   Interfacing an ultrasonic transmitter
to the computer printer port*

For the programs suggested in this book you need to load a version of BASIC, such as GWBASIC or QUICKBASIC. You can also adapt the following programs to other languages such as C and PASCAL.

In BASIC, the command for sending (or writing) a data byte to an output port is:

OUT address, value

We are using bit 0 of register 03BC so the command is:

112

OUT &H03BC, 1

The &H signifies to BASIC that the following number is in hexadecimal. Since the 'value' 1 is the same in decimal or hexadecimal, there is no need for the &H in the 'value'. Here is a program to flash the LED once:

```
10    REM ** High pulse 1 **
20    OUT &H03BC,0
30    GOSUB 80
40    OUT &H03BC,1
50    GOSUB 80
60    OUT &H03BC,0
70    STOP
80    FOR J = 1 TO 10000:NEXT
90    RETURN
```

Type this in *exactly* as it is printed and RUN it. Remember to distinguish between '0' (zero) and 'O' (letter 'oh'). The LED flashes once. If the IR LEDs are directed towards a receiver with a controlled device attached, it should show the expected response. Let us look at this program more closely, to see how it works. When we refer to 'the LED' In the description we mean both the visible LED and the invisible IR LED(s).

Line 10 begins with REM which tells the computer to ignore anything following on that line. We have used it to place a title on the program for our own information. Line 20 is the output statement referred to above, and sends a '0' to pin 2. The effect of this is to make the pin go to a logical 'low' level if it was not already in that state. The 'low' level turns Q1 off. This is really a precaution just in case the pin was left high at the end of a previous program. Line 30 sends the computer to a subroutine at line 80. Here the value of variable J is counted up from 1 to 10000, an operation which delays the running of the program, giving us time to see that the LED is off. Line 90 returns the computer to the place at which it left the main program and the command at line 40 turns the LED on. Now the computer jumps to the subroutine for another delay to give us time to see that the LED is on, and time for the receiver, if any, to respond. On returning to line 60, the computer is commanded to turn the

LED off, ending the pulse. Line 70 ends the program. With this simple program we have a way of remotely controlling any of the projects that use a single-pulse transmitter with an IR channel.

The program above is not entirely convenient, because you have to type RUN and press ENTER or RETURN each time you want to send a pulse. The program below works repeatedly:

```
10    REM ** High Pulse 2 **
20    CLS: OUT &H03BC, 0
30    IF INKEY$ = "" THEN 30
40    OUT &H03BC,1
50    GOSUB 80
60    OUT &H03BC,0
70    GOTO 30
80    FOR J = 1 TO 10000:NEXT
90    RETURN
```

Line 10 is a REM, as before. Line 20 clears the screen, and makes the bit 'low', just in case it has been left 'high'. The computer cycles indefinitely in line 30 waiting for a key (any key) to be pressed. Note that there are two quote symbols with no space between them. This is the BASIC way of representing 'no key pressed'. From line 40 onward the program is as before, except that, instead of stopping at line 70, the computer is sent back to line 30 to wait for the next key-press. For this program you have to type RUN only once. After that, the computer sends a pulse every time you press a key. The program may be used with any of the toggling devices and devices which step through a number of stages each time they receive a pulse. There is a chance for you to add text to this program by using the PRINT command. For example, you could insert:

35 PRINT "Pulse sent"

Or you could devise a way of displaying on the screen the present state of the controlled device.

One of the difficulties of operating the multiple-pulse devices by hand is counting the pulses. It is all too easy to overstep the stage and have to run round all the stages again to get to the right one. Here is a program that overcomes this problem:

```
10   REM ** Pulser **
20   OUT &H03BC, 0: pulses = 7
30   CLS
40   INPUT "Key the number of steps";n
50   IF n<1 OR n>pulses THEN GOTO 30
60   FOR k = 1 to n
70   OUT &H03BC,1
80   GOSUB 130
90   OUT &H03BC,0
100  GOSUB 130
110  NEXT k
120  GOTO 30
130  FOR J = 1 TO 10000:NEXT
140  RETURN
```

The variable 'pulses' is the number of stages in the system less one; in other words this is number of pulses needed to go once around the cycle but stopping short of the starting stage. The value 7 is for an 8-stage device. Alter 'pulses' to suit your controlled device before saving the program. Line 40 asks how many steps (= how many pulses). Line 50 checks that the number keyed in is acceptable and, if not, asks for the number to be re-entered. Lines 60 to 110 are a FOR...NEXT loop which generates a pulse each time round, making n pulses (each high followed by low) altogether. Then the computer returns to line 40 to await fresh instructions.

Finally, here is a more sophisticated program that calculates how many pulses are needed to get from one stage to another and generates the required number of pulses:

```
10   REM ** Stage finder **
20   OUT &H03BC, 0: stages = 7: place = 0
30   CLS
40   INPUT "Key the stage required";s
50   IF s<0 OR s>stages THEN GOTO 30
```

```
 60    pulses = s - place
 70    if pulses <0 then pulses = pulses + stages
 80    FOR k = 1 to pulses
 90    OUT &H03BC,1
100    GOSUB 160
110    OUT &H03BC,0
120    GOSUB 160
130    NEXT k
140    place = s
150    GOTO 30
160    FOR J = 1 TO 10000:NEXT
170    RETURN
```

Now we are beginning to make fuller use of computer power. It is possible to design a logic circuit to perform this operation but such a circuit requires several ics and careful construction and testing. Software is so much simpler to handle. In this program, 'stages' is the number of the last stage (the first stage being stage 0) so the listing above is for an 8-stage device. We assume that the device is in stage 0 to begin with, so 'place' (the number of the current stage) is set to zero in line 20. Subsequently (line 140) it is updated as we move from stage to stage. Line 40 asks the user to key in the number of the stage to which the device is to go. Lines 50 to 70 calculate how many pulses are needed to do this. Lines 80 to 130 are a loop to transmit the pulses. After this line 140 registers the new place, and line 150 sends the computer back to await new instructions.

Remotely Controlling the Computer
One of the IR or ultrasonic receivers may be connected to the printer port as shown in Figure 4.12. The power supply to the receiver must be either a 5V regulated supply or a 6V battery. The 4.7V Zener diode limits the voltage applied to the port. For a 1-bit input, which will be enough for receiving single-pulse and multiple-pulse inputs, we will use bit 0 of register 03BE. The command for reading from a register is:

$$A = INP(address)$$

A is a variable which is then assigned the present value in the register. Because we are interested only in bit 0, we discount the

116

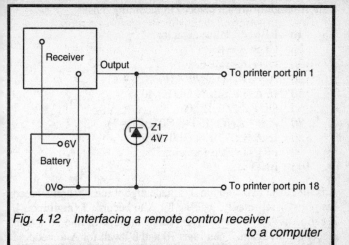

Fig. 4.12   Interfacing a remote control receiver
to a computer

other bits by ANDing A with 0001:

$$A = 1 \text{ AND INP}(\&03BE)$$

A further slight complication is that bit 0 (and also bits 1 and 3) are inverted. It makes programs easier to understand if we convert A into 1 if it is 0 and into 0 if it is 1. This is easily done by adding 1 to the input. The effect of this on the other bits is ignored since we AND out all except bit 0:

$$A = 1 \text{ AND (INP}(\&03BE) + 1)$$

The routine for obtaining input is to first make bit 0 high then, if it is receiving a high input, it will remain high. On the other hand, it is pulled low if it is receiving a low input. The input register is rather more complicated than using the output register but, since we are dealing with only a single bit, it is just a matter of getting used to this standard routine:

```
OUT &H03BE, 0
A = 1 AND (INP(&03BE) + 1)
```

The first line sets bit 0 to high by sending a zero to the register (remember the bit is inverted). Then A returns the value 0 if the input is 'low' or 1 if the input is 'high'. We are now ready to use

117

a short program which detects an incoming pulse:

```
10   REM ** Pulse detector **
20   CLS: A = 0
30   OUT &H03BE, 0
40   A = 1 AND (INP(&H03BE) + 1)
50   IF A = 0 THEN GOTO 40
60   OUT &H03BE, 0
70   A = 1 AND (INP(&H03BE) + 1)
80   IF A = 1 THEN GOTO 70
90   PRINT "Pulse received"
100  END
```

A is first reset to 0, and pin 0 is made high. Lines 40 and 50 read the register repeatedly, waiting for A to become 1 (high input). As soon as A = 1, the program drops through to line 60 which resets the bit again. Then lines 70 and 80 wait for A to become 0, indicating the end of the pulse. As soon as A = 0, the program drops through to line 90 to display the message. In a practical program line 90 could be the beginning of a routine to perform a particular function, perhaps to send output to a controlled device. The connections between input and output are a matter of programming.

For multiple pulse systems we need a program to count the number of pulses received:

```
10   REM ** Pulse counter **
20   CLS: A = 0: n = 0:delay = 5
30   OUT &H03BE, 0
40   A = 1 AND (INP(&H03BE) + 1)
50   IF A = 0 THEN GOTO 40
60   OUT &H03BE, 0
70   A = 1 AND (INP(&H03BE) + 1)
80   IF A = 1 THEN GOTO 70
90   n = n+1
100  OUT &H03BE, 0
110  ft = VAL(RIGHT$(TIME$,2)) + delay
120  IF ft>59 THEN ft = ft - 60
130  A = 1 AND (INP(&H03BE) + 1)
140  IF A = 0 AND VAL(RIGHT$(TIME$,2))< ft
     THEN GOTO 130
```

118

```
150   IF A = 1 THEN GOTO 70
160   PRINT " The number of pulses is ";n
170   n = 0:GOTO 30
180   END
```

In this program, n is the number of pulses counted; delay is the number of seconds the computer is to wait after the end of a pulse before it decides that there are no more pulses arriving in that group. We have set delay to 5, but this is easily altered by editing line 20. Input is 'low' to begin with. Lines 30 and 40 make the computer wait until input goes 'high', that is, the first pulse arrives. Lines 70 and 80 keep the computer waiting until input goes 'low', the pulse has ended. Line 90 counts the number of pulses so far. Line 110 calculates a value for ft, the finishing time when the computer is to give up waiting for further pulses. This is calculated by reading the right-hand two digits of TIME$, which gives the hours, minutes and seconds currently registered on the computer's clock. RIGHT$ slices off the two right-most characters (the seconds) and VAL converts these to a number, to which we add the delay. Lines 130 and 140 form a loop in which the computer waits until input goes high (another pulse arrives) or the finishing time is reached. If another pulse has arrived (line 150) the program jumps to line 70 and waits for the pulse to end. Otherwise the finishing time has been reached (Line 160) and the number of pulses is displayed. In line 170, n is reset to zero and the program jumps to line 30, ready to receive the next group of pulses. This is simply a pulse counting program but it could be extended after line 160 to jump to various routines (including outputs to controlled devices) depending on the value of n, before returning to line 30 to wait for the next group.

Many electronic devices including DC motors, stepper motors, relays, solenoids and different kinds of sensor, may be interfaced to the computer to build up a computerised remote control system. For further details, consult BP 377, *Practical Electronic Control Projects*.

The BASIC Stamp Microcontroller

Because of their small size and low power requirements, microcontrollers are particularly suitable for portable control systems. They may have limited memory but remote control usually involves only short programs, which are easily stored in a small memory. The Stamp microcontroller is small in other ways too. It is assembled on a pcb measuring only 35mm × 10mm (the BS1 version). When quiescent, it takes only 20µA so that it can run for days or even weeks from a 9V PP3 battery.

The Stamp has the advantage that it is programmable in BASIC. The Stamp's version of BASIC includes most of the standard BASIC commands and also some special ones related to its use as a microcontroller. There is room in its 256 byte ROM for about 80 program lines, which is more than enough for practically all remote control applications. The ROM is an electrically erasable programmable ROM (EEPROM). Once the Stamp has been programmed (this is done on a PC, then downloaded) it retains the program indefinitely after the power has been turned off. There are also 16 bytes of RAM for data storage. The Stamp is accompanied by a handbook, a disc with the programming software and many sample programs, a connector to the printer port of a PC, and a carrier board on which there is a prototyping area. Additional Stamps are available at a reasonably low price.

The Handbook supplied with the Stamp contains full instructions for programming and using the ic, as well as several applications notes and programs. In this section we deal with the application of the Stamp to remote control projects. At the testing stage you will probably prefer to set up a project on a breadboard instead of on the prototyping area, reserving this for assembling the perfected circuit later. Either make up a 14-pin single-in-line socket to fit on to the 14-pin plug of the carrier board and take the wires from this to a breadboard, or solder the connecting wires directly into the row of holes that run beside the 14-pin plug. The Stamp may be powered from a 5V DC regulated supply applied to the V_{dd} pin. More often in remote control applications, it is preferable to use a battery. The battery voltage should be in the range 6V to 15V, and is applied to the V_{in} pin. Often a PP3 9V battery will provide sufficient power and is a compact source suited to mobile projects. It can be plugged directly into the pair of spring terminals on the Stamp's mother-board. When a battery is used, the built-in regulator of the Stamp provides a regulated 5V supply from its

V_dd pin. This is useful when controlling certain logic circuits which require 5V. The output pins can provide up to 20mA each, which is enough to drive an LED or a remote control transmitter directly. As inputs, they can sink up to 25mA each. But, if you are using several pins simultaneously, the total current sunk must not be more than 50mA, and the total sourced must not be more than 40mA.

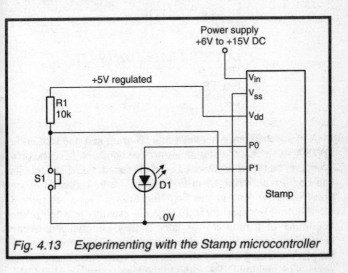

Fig. 4.13   Experimenting with the Stamp microcontroller

The main application of the Stamp in a remote control transmitter is to generate a sequence of pulses. There is nothing to be gained by using it to replace the logic of Figure 2.1 or Figure 2.6, but you could consider using it instead of the MV500 and other coder ics. The Stamp manual contains application notes on setting up an infra-red communication system which could be the basis of a remote control system in which both the transmitter and receiver are built around Stamps. As an introduction to the Stamp and to help make you familiar with its BASIC, we describe here a few much simpler systems. We begin with a program for use when the Stamp is connected as in Figure 4.13 and which generates a single pulse when a button is pressed. Figure 4.13 shows the connections required for the first experimental program listed below. Input is provided by a push-button S1 connected to pin 1. Normally pin 1 is held high by R1 which is connected to the 5V line. This ensures that the input voltage can not exceed 5V. The output from pin 0 goes directly to an LED. Since the output current is limited to 20mA (see below) there is no need for a resistor in series with the LED. Here is the experimental program:

```
'Single pulse
DIRS = %11111101
B2=0
WAIT:
BUTTON 1,0,255,0,B2,0,WAIT
HIGH 0
PAUSE 1000
LOW 0
GOTO WAIT
```

A major difference between this program and one written in GWBASIC is that the Stamp has no line numbers. Also the program can be typed in lower case, if preferred. REM statements can begin with REM, as in GWBASIC, or be preceded by an apostrophe (') as in the first line above. There are only 8 input/output pins and their direction is usually specified at the beginning of a program, or later if they are changed. Some commands automatically change the direction before executing. In the listing above, all pins except pin 1 are specified as outputs by making DIRS equal to the binary number 11111101, the preceding % indicating that this is a binary number. The zero makes pin 1 an input.

Next comes the *address* label WAIT:, which marks a point in the program to which the microcontroller jumps when instructed. The label can be any word we choose, except a keyword or variable, and must be followed by a colon to define it as a label. The Stamp does not actually wait at WAIT:, but continues to the next statement, the BUTTON command. This is a rather complicated command as it has 7 parameters, each of which is used to specify exactly what is to happen at this stage. Taking them in order the parameters used in the program above mean:

The *pin* to read is pin 1

The *downstate* is 0, which tells the Stamp that pressing the

122

button gives a *low* input.

The *delay*, when set to 255 as above, simply debounces the button, with no auto-repeat

The *auto-repeat rate* is zero (there is no auto-repeat)

The *byte variable* is B2, already cleared for use as the button's work-space

The *target state* is 0. The target state tells the Stamp what state of the button to look for; 0 = pressed, 1 = not pressed; in this example it looks for 0, which means it checks that the button is not pressed.

The *address* to branch to if the button is in the target state is WAIT.

For as long as the button is not pressed the program loops back to WAIT. As soon as the button is pressed the Stamp continues to the remainder of the program. It makes output 0 go high, which switches on the LED. Then there is a pause for 1000ms (= 1 second) after which it makes output 0 go low, turning off the LED. Finally, GOTO WAIT sends the Stamp back to WAIT, to wait for you to press the button again. The result is that the LED goes high for 1 second every time you press the button.

Once the program has been typed into the PC, with the Stamp connected to the computer, RUN it. It is downloaded into the Stamp and runs immediately. If all is in order, you may then disconnect the Stamp from the computer. The program runs again whenever you press the Reset button on the carrier board. It also runs when you switch the power on.

Such a program is of little practical value since you can obtain 1-second pulses very easily just by using Figure 2.5 and holding down the button for an estimated 1 second. The aim is to introduce a few BASIC commands, to give you the experience of loading and running a program, and to check that your system is working properly.

The following program is more useful. It produces a specified number of pulses, according to which button is pressed. This is useful for sequential systems such as Figure 3.5 and Figure 3.8. Figure 4.14 shows a circuit for controlling a 4-stage system such as Figure 3.8. If you want fewer stages, omit the buttons not required. If you want more stages (up to 7), simply

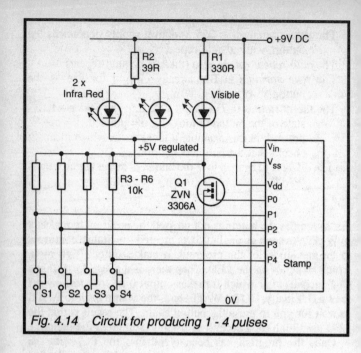

Fig. 4.14   Circuit for producing 1 - 4 pulses

add more buttons.

```
'Sequential pulses
DIRS = %11100001
LOW 0
START:
IF PIN4 = 0 OR PIN3 = 0 OR PIN2 = 0 OR PIN1 = 0
    THEN START
WHICH:
IF PIN4 = 0 THEN FOUR
IF PIN3 = 0 THEN THREE
IF PIN2 = 0 THEN TWO
IF PIN1 = 0 THEN ONE
GOTO WHICH
FOUR:
    GOSUB PULSE
THREE:
```

```
        GOSUB PULSE
TWO:
        GOSUB PULSE
ONE:
        GOSUB PULSE
GOTO START
PULSE:
        HIGH 0
        PAUSE 100
        LOW 0
        PAUSE 100
        RETURN
```

The DIRS command makes pins 1 to 4 inputs. Then we read the state of the inputs to all four pins in turn, using the PIN command. The compound OR statement ensures that if any one or more of the pins is already pressed the Stamp is sent back to START, to interrogate the keys again. It continues in this way until none of the keys are pressed. It then drops down to the next routine in which each key is interrogated in turn to find which one is subsequently pressed. For as long as no keys are pressed, the program cycles in a loop returning every time to WHICH. But if any key is pressed it jumps out of the loop, to addresses FOUR, THREE, TWO, or ONE. If for example, key 4 is pressed it jumps to FOUR. This sends it to the PULSE subroutine, to produce one pulse. We have made this only 0.1s long in this program, which is usually long enough for sequential pulses. After the pulse there is a 0.1s delay, then the RETURN command sends the STAMP back to the point it jumped from, and it continues to THREE. There it is sent to the subroutine again to produce another pulse. In turn, it goes to TWO and then ONE, producing a pulse each time, a total of four pulses. But if, for example key 2 is pressed instead of key 4, the Stamp is sent directly to TWO, and produces only two pulses before it reaches the end of the chain. At the end of the chain it is sent back to START. Here it waits until no key is pressed before is begins interrogating the keyboard again. This is an essential feature of the program because it gives the operator time to release the pressed key before pressing the next key. Note that, if two or more keys are pressed simultaneously, the highest-numbered one is read and the others are ignored.

A Stamp loaded with this sequential pulse program can be used to control any of the sequential systems described earlier in the book. It can also be used with a receiver to which is connected another Stamp running a pulse-counting program, such as this:

```
'Pulse counter
DIRS = %11111110
SYMBOL COUNT = 0
WAIT:
        IF PIN0 = 0 THEN WAIT
REPEAT:
        LET COUNT = COUNT + 1
IF COUNT = 4 THEN FINISH
PAUSE 210
IF PIN0 = 1 THEN REPEAT
FINISH:
HIGH COUNT
PAUSE 100
LOW COUNT
COUNT = 0
GOTO WAIT
```

The operation of this program depends on the signal consisting of 1 to 4 pulses, each 0.1s long, with 0.1s gaps between them. It can readily be adapted to other numbers of pulses and different timings. The first line after the title defines pin 0 as an input and the other pins (1-4) as outputs. The next line defines a variable called COUNT, in which the number of pulses received is stored and which to begin with is set to 0. The program waits in a loop, returning to WAIT for as long as pin 0 is low (no signal). As soon as the first pulse arrives and pin 0 is made high, the program drops through and increments COUNT to 1. There is then a pause of 0.21s. This gives time for the input to go low at the end of the pulse, remain low for 0.1s and then, if another pulse arrives to go high again. The next line tests pin 0 to see what has happened. If the pin is high, a second pulse has arrived so the program loops back to increment COUNT to 2. If pin 0 is still low the sequence of pulses has ended. It drops through to send an output pulse to the appropriate pin. We use the commands HIGH pin and LOW pin, in which pin is the number of the pin to be made high or low, which in this example is simply COUNT, the number counted. In this way one of pins 1 to 4 is made high for 1 second and causes the appropriate action to occur. It might directly turn on a transistor switch to control, say a lamp, siren or other device. Or it might be used logically to trigger a flip-flop which turns on a device and leaves it on until a pulse from another pin triggers it off again. After the pulse has been delivered, COUNT is made 0 again and the program loops back to WAIT for the next sequence of pulses. Note that the line 'IF COUNT = 4 THEN FINISH' takes the Stamp directly to making pin 4 go high without waiting to see if there are any further pulses. This guards against the possibility of a second train of pulses following immediately after the first causing COUNT to increase to 5 or more.

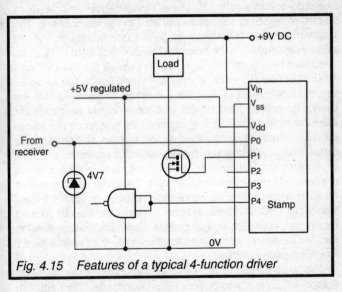

Fig. 4.15   Features of a typical 4-function driver

Figure 4.15 shows a circuit suitable for use with this program. It is powered by a 9V battery, although any battery in the range 6V to 15V could be used. Input to pin 0 comes from a receiver circuit, such as Figures 2.2 or 2.7. Or it may come by cable using line drivers and receivers, as in Figures 2.8 to 2.12. The Zener diode is required only if the high output from the receiver exceeds 5V. The figure shows two examples of output circuitry. Pin 1 drives a MOSFET switch which switches on a load, such as an LED, a filament lamp, motor or relay. These are powered directly from the 9V battery. Pin 4 drives a logic gate powered from the 5V regulated line. This is used for any other ics for which a 5V regulated supply is essential. However, CMOS and 74HC logic can be powered directly from the battery. Chapter 5 provides suggestions for switches and other circuits that can be driven from the Stamp's output pins.

Project 13 – Remote Temperature Reading

This project differs from the others in that the controlling unit operates automatically. It senses temperature and sends a stream of pulses at a frequency related to the temperature. The receiver converts this stream of pulses into a voltage, voltage being proportional to frequency. Thus the controlled device is a voltmeter but, since a voltage can be used as the basis of subsequent action it would be easy to extend the circuit to drive, say, the motor of an electric fan. Like most of the projects in the book, this one or parts of this one are so easily adaptable for other functions. Another way in which the project can be adapted is to substitute some other sensor, such as a photodiode or piezo-electric strain gauge for the temperature sensor.

Another way of looking at this project is to take it as an example of *remote sensing*, in which the sensor is in a remote location which might be impossible, difficult or simply inconvenient to visit. The readout is on a meter conveniently located in, say, the workshop or living room. One particular application for this circuit is in the greenhouse; with the readout meter handily situated indoors.

The transmitter (Fig. 4.16) consists of the temperature sensor (IC1), which as described in Project 4, produces an output voltage proportional to the Celsius temperature. An op amp amplifies this voltage tenfold but since this is an inverting amplifier, its output is fed to a second op amp (IC3)

128

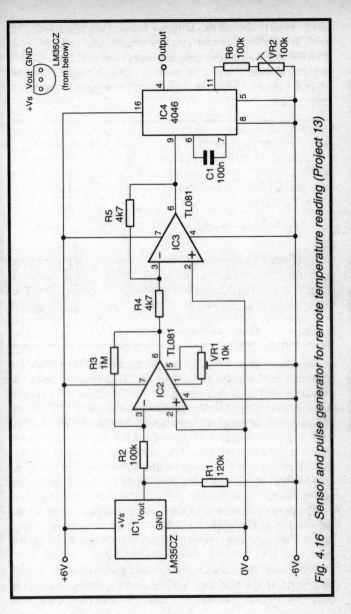

Fig. 4.16 Sensor and pulse generator for remote temperature reading (Project 13)

129

which inverts the signal without further amplification. The result is a voltage proportional to temperature and swinging from 0V to 4V as temperature increases from 0°C to 40°C. It is possible to alter R3 to give greater or lesser amplification to adapt the circuit to operate with a smaller or greater maximum temperature.

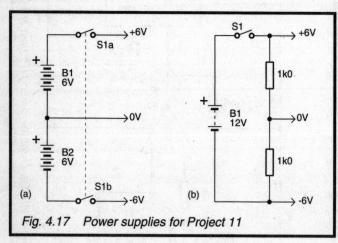

Fig. 4.17   Power supplies for Project 11

The circuit is powered by two 6V batteries (Fig. 4.17a) or a regulated ±6V supply. The use of the 7660 inverting ic is not recommended as in this circuit we need to know the negative voltage accurately. Another possibility is to use a 12V battery and use a pair of equal resistors to feed the 0V line (Fig. 4.17b). This is a little wasteful of current since 6mA out of the total 20mA required for this circuit flows through the two 1kΩ resistors. A circuit powered as in Figure 4.17b may also use a 9V PP3 battery, which is suitable for intermittent use. It then takes about 10mA.

The preset potentiometer VR1 serves to adjust the input offset voltage of the amplifier. When the circuit is being tested, adjust VR1 so that the output of IC3 is 0V (relative to the 0V line)

The output from the second op amp goes to the phase-lock loop ic (IC4) in which we are using only the voltage-controlled oscillator (VCO). The centre frequency f_0 of the oscillator is given by:

$$f_o = 1/RC$$

where R is the combined resistance of R6 and VR2. If VR2 is set to make their combined resistance 200kΩ, the output frequency of IC4 is 50Hz when the input voltage is half the supply voltage. Note that IC4 is powered from the +6V and –6V lines, so its supply voltage is 12V. Half that voltage is 6V which, *relative to the –6V line*, is the voltage of the 0V line. Thus when the temperature is 0°C and the output of IC3 is 0V (relative to the 0V line), the output frequency of IC4 is 50Hz. It rises toward a maximum of 100Hz as the input to pin 9 rises to +6V. However the output of a TL081 op amp is not able to rise to its supply rail, so that frequency will not be reached.

The output of IC4 could be fed to a MOSFET switch which flashes IR LEDs at the appropriate frequency. But in the applications in which this circuit is more likely to be used there would be an optical fibre or a direct wire connection to the receiver. Line driving ics (Chapter 2) will be required if the connection is lengthy.

The project is also suitable for use with a radio link, making it a practical example of radio telemetry. The output of IC4 is fed to pin 14 of an MC145026. In the receiver the decoder is an MC145028 with its 'valid message' output (pin 11) wired to the frequency-to-voltage converter, as in Figure 4.18. The centre frequency of 50Hz rec ommended for IR and cable connection is rather too rapid for use with systems which include the MC145026/8 ics. The transmission of two code groups does not allow time for a gap between pulses. It is better to reduce the centre frequency to around 10Hz, by making R6 (Fig. 4.16) equal to 820kΩ and increasing VR2 to 250kΩ.

The receiver (possibly with an IR receiver as its first stage) is shown in Figure 4.18. It is connected in the same way as in Fig 4.5 but here it is driving a meter. The output voltage is:

$$V_{OUT} = F_{IN} \times 7.56RC$$

where R is the combined resistance of R10 and VR3, and C is the capacitance of C4. If VR3 is set to make the combined resistance of R10 and VR3 equal to 820kΩ, the output voltage at 0°C is:

$$V_0 = 50 \times 7.65 \times 820 \times 10^3 \times 10 \times 10^{-9} = 3.1365\text{V}$$

As temperature rises, the voltage increases. As temperature falls below 0°C the voltage falls. It is not easy to calculate exactly what reading to expect at a given temperature as the response of IC4 is not perfectly linear and the op amp outputs are non-linear as they approach extremes. The best technique is to calibrate the system by measuring the output voltage when the sensor is placed in situations at a number of different temperatures. At the same time, measure the temperature with an ordinary direct-reading thermometer. However, before doing this you should set the full scale deflection (f.s.d.) as described below.

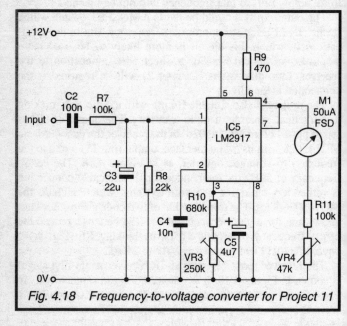

Fig. 4.18   Frequency-to-voltage converter for Project 11

In Figure 4.18 the op amp output goes to a microammeter, which is made to act as a voltmeter by connecting a resistor in series with it. The meter shown has a full-scale deflection of 50μA so we need to calculate suitable values for the series resistance so that the meter will show full-scale deflection when the temperature is at the maximum that we wish to read. Suppose that the maximum temperature to be read is 40°C and that this produces an output of 5.5V from IC5. If a 5.5V output is to produce a current of 50μA, the total resistance of R11, VR4 *and the coil of the meter* must be:

$$R = V/I = 5.5/(50 \times 10^{-6}) = 110k\Omega$$

If the resistance of the coil is 3.5kΩ, the combined resistance of R11 and VR4 must be 110kΩ – 3.5kΩ = 106.5kΩ. This setting can be obtained with the values shown in Figure 4.18. If you have a different maximum voltage, or a meter with a different f.s.d. current, or a different coil resistance, you may need to substitute other values for R11 and VR4. When setting up the circuit, place the sensor where it is at the maximum temperature. Allow a few seconds for the output of IC5 to settle (it does not change instantly), then adjust VR4 to bring the needle to the maximum scale reading. After that, you can proceed to calibrate it as described above.

Project 14 – Proportional Control, Using the Stamp

This is to a certain extent an experimental project as you may have to play around with component values to obtain the result you require. But is it also a project with many possible applications, and the applications we leave to you. Essentially, the controller unit has a rotary potentiometer which can be turned to any position on a marked scale. The controlled device includes the Stamp and this produces an output voltage ranging from 0V to 5V as the potentiometer knob traverses its scale. You may use a slider potentiometer or a joystick (see Fig. 4.1) instead of the rotary potentiometer. There are numerous ways of exploiting the varying output voltage: controlling the speed of a motor, the brightness of a lamp, the frequency of a VCO or the volume of sound (Fig. 4.8) from an amplifier.

The controller uses the circuit illustrated in Figure 5.15. There the component values are intended for use with a standard servo-control ic which requires a pulse ranging in length from 1ms to 2ms, produced every 18ms. In this application, the frequency (or frame) does not have to be exact, so VR1 may be omitted.

The circuit for the controlled device (Fig. 4.19) is very simple. Input comes from an IR receiver, a line receiver or a direct cable link and may need a 4.7V or 5.1V Zener diode to limit it. The input goes to pin 0 and the program measures the length of the pulse, using the Stamp's PULSIN command. Then the Stamp produces a pulse-width-modulation output on pin 1. As explained in the manual, this is a mixture of 0's and 1's, ranging from all 0's to produce zero voltage across the capacitor, to all 1's to produce 5V across the capacitor. The voltage across the capacitor can be used directly for device driving, provided that the device has high-impedance input (that is, it draws virtually no current). With most devices it is necessary to use a buffer wired as a voltage follower, as in the figure. This could, of course be replaced by a voltage amplifier if you want to produce an output range greater than 0V–5V.

Here are the essentials of the program; this is likely to be only part of a rather larger program but is sufficient for testing the system.

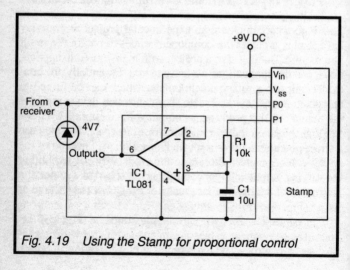

Fig. 4.19   Using the Stamp for proportional control

```
'Proportional control sample:
PULSIN 0, 1, b0
LET b0 = b0 - 100 MIN 0
LET b1 = b0 * 2
LET b2 = b0 / 2
LET b0 = b0 / 20
LET b0 = b0 + b1 + b2 MAX 255
PWM 1, b0, 20
GOTO sample
```

There is no need for a DIRS statement as the PULSIN and PWM commands automatically set the pin to input and output, respectively. PULSIN has three parameters: the 0 specifies pin 0, the 1 instructs the Stamp to wait for a rising edge (start of a pulse) before commencing timing, b0 instructs the Stamp to store the length of the pulse (reckoned in 10µs intervals) in byte b0. The result will be a value in b0 ranging between 100 (equivalent to the scale minimum, 0) and 200 (the scale maximum).

Now, in 5 lines, we process b0 to convert it from a value ranging from 100 to 200, to a value ranging from 0 to 255. Remember that the Stamp processes all mathematical statements strictly from left to right. In the first line, b0 has 100 subtracted from it and, in case this results in a negative number (supposing the controller is running slightly fast, or a noisy environment ends the pulse prematurely) the minimum possible value is 0. Next b0 is multiplied by 2 and the result stored in b1. In the next line b0 is divided by 2 and the result is stored in b2. Finally b0 is divided by 20 and the result stored in b0. After this, we add b2 and b1 to b0. The MAX command ensures that the result does not exceed 255. In effect, these three lines have subtracted 100 from b0 and multiplied the result by 2.55, but the Stamp's BASIC does not allow for floating-point operations so we have had to use integer methods.

Now we output the stream of 0's and 1's it produces, using the PWM command. The parameters of this statement are as follows: 1 directs the output to pin 1, b1 identifies the data to be used to generate the bit stream, 20 instructs Stamp to generate 20 cycles of the bit stream. The voltage produced is $255/b1 \times 5$, so the output voltage ranges from 0V to 5V. The number of cycles determines to what extent the voltage across the capacitor reaches the required value. There are certain to be leakages of charge and this can be compensated for by increasing the number of cycles. Or you may find that this number can be reduced without adversely affecting the result.

This project serves to illustrate what can be done with the PULSIN and PWM commands as well as how to handle calculations in integer arithmetic. For more advanced projects, many of which are adaptable to remote control applications, refer to the Stamp handbook.

Chapter 5

DRIVERS

To assist the designer of remote control projects, this chapter collects driving circuits used in various projects in the book and looks at them systematically. First we describe ways of switching devices on and off. Then we go on to look at certain devices in more detail.

Switching

A few devices can be switched directly from the output of a logic gate or from the outputs of an ic such as a counter. A CMOS ic can supply up to 0.16mA with a 'high' output level and when the supply voltage is 5V. At 10V it can supply up to 0.4mA and at 15V it can supply up to 1.2mA. CMOS buffers (inverting 4049, non-inverting 4050) can supply slightly larger currents of 2.5mA, 2.6mA and 10mA respectively at the three supply voltages. The various versions of the 74 series can supply rather higher currents, but no logic gates are capable of driving more than a standard LED (weakly lit) or a ultraminiature relay. A device that has useful driving power is the 7555 timer with a maximum output of 100mA, plenty enough to drive a small relay or a small filament lamp. Use the older 555 version for outputs up to 200mA.

Transistor Switches

More often we switch a load on by using a transistor driven into saturation. Figure 5.1a shows the basic circuit, for switching by *bipolar junction transistors*. The current available at the collector terminal of a BJT depends on how much current the transistor can safely conduct when switched fully on. In Figure 5.1a , all current passing through the load also passes through the transistor. The maximum current allowed is a few hundred milliamps if the transistor is of the low-power type, such as a BC548 (100mA), BC109 (high gain, 100mA), or ZTX300 (500mA). If a greater current is required, simply substitute a BJT of higher rating. Examples are the BD131 (3A) and the 2N3055 (15A). The circuit in Figure 5.1a powers the load when

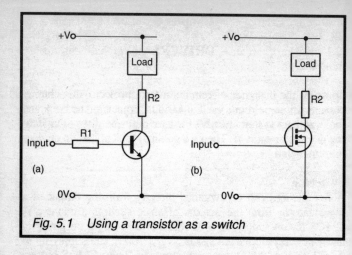

Fig. 5.1   Using a transistor as a switch

the transistor is switched on by a input greater than about 1V. The value of the input resistor R1 can be calculated from R1 = $\beta \times (V_{ON} - 0.6)/I_{LOAD}$, where β is the gain of the transistor (take this to be 100 if you can not find it in the data tables), V_{ON} is the input voltage at which the load it to be turned on and I_{LOAD} is the maximum current through the load. Use the next standard resistor below the calculated value. R2 is required only if the load is not rated to withstand the full supply voltage. You might need it when switching LEDs and low-voltage torch lamps, or small motors and relays. Calculate R2 from:

$$R2 = (V_{SUPPLY} - V_{MAX} - 0.6)/I_{LOAD}$$

V_{MAX} is the maximum voltage at which the load is rated to operate.

The alternative to a BJT is the *n-channel enhancement mode MOSFET* (Fig. 5.1b). In general we prefer this because (a) present-day power MOSFETs have a very low 'on' resistance, (b) the gate current is virtually nil, which means that (c) the input resistor R1 is unnecessary. R2 is calculated as above. The circuit in Figure 5.1b powers the load when the transistor is switched on by a input greater than the gate threshold voltage, which is about 3V. There are many MOSFETs suitable for

138

switching. Examples are ZVN4306A (1.3A, 0.33Ω, 3V), the IRF630 (9A, 0.33Ω, 2V to 4V) and the BUZ11 (30A, 0.03Ω, 2.1V to 4V); the figures in brackets are the maximum drain current, the 'on' resistance and the threshold gate voltage.

Sometimes it is necessary to switch a load that requires a voltage higher than is acceptable for the rest of the circuit. Figure 5.2 shows how the load may be connected to the higher voltage while the remainder of the circuit operates on a lower supply voltage (+V).

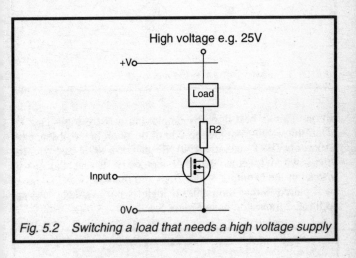

Fig. 5.2   Switching a load that needs a high voltage supply

A precaution must be taken when switching inductive loads, such as relays, solenoids, motors, bells, and buzzers (not the so-called solid-state buzzers). When the current is switched off, the sudden collapse of the magnetic field in the coil of the load causes a high reverse voltage to be induced in the coil. This may be several hundred volts in size. It can easily destroy the switching transistor in an instant. To guard against this we connect a diode across the load, as in Figure 5.3. This discharges the reverse energy safely. Some devices, especially relays, are manufactured with the diode already present.

All the switching circuits described so far switch the load on when the input rises. Sometimes we may require the opposite

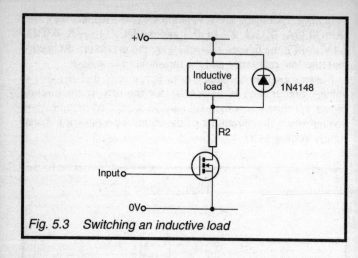

Fig. 5.3 Switching an inductive load

action. This is best done by employing a spare logic gate to invert the signal from the receiver or decoder. In the absence of a spare INVERT gate, use a NAND gate or a NOR gate with its inputs wired together. Another method is to use the Q-bar instead of the Q output of flip-flops and other devices that have such paired output terminals. If logic is not available, use an additional transistor, as in Figure 5.4.

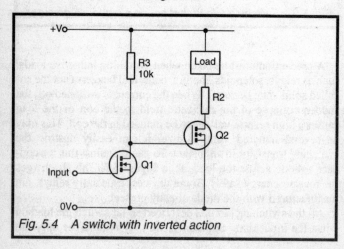

Fig. 5.4 A switch with inverted action

Quite often we need to provide several switches and the wiring of the required number of transistors is not only tedious but also takes up valuable board space. There are ics such as the ULN2001N which contains an array of identical switching circuits. Figure 5.5 explains how to use this ic for switching up to 8 devices. The switching is done by Darlington transistors, so only a small input current is required for each. Each switch incorporates a diode so inductive loads do not require the diode shown in Figure 5.3. The cathode terminals of all eight diodes are taken to a common terminal (pin 9) so there is only one connection to be made to the +V line, another simplification of the wiring.

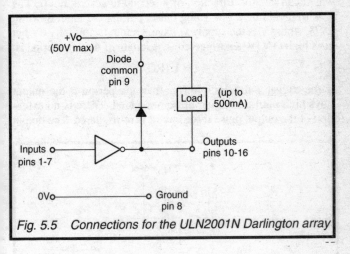

Fig. 5.5 Connections for the ULN2001N Darlington array

A switching transistor dissipates power, the amount depending on the collector-emitter or drain-source pd and the current. Thus there is no dissipation when the transistor is off and relatively little when it is fully on (especially with MOSFETs with low 'on' resistances). But when switching from 'off' to 'on and back again, dissipation is higher. If a transistor is actively switching on and off at high frequency its power dissipation can be quite high. The situation is remedied by fitting a heat sink or bolting the transistor to a heat sink. Obviously a heat-sink is a nuisance in portable equipment because heat sinks take up space and increase the weight of the equipment. But they must be fitted if required. The best approach is to observe how hot the transistor gets when the circuit is operating and fit heat sinks where necessary.

One point about transistor switching is that this can be used only for direct current. If the load requires AC, you must use a relay, as described later.

Timed Switches

Often it is convenient if a single pulse switches on a controlled device for a preset period of time. The circuit in Figure 5.6 uses the 7555 timer ic to turn on a controlled device for a period which can last for a fraction of a second to several hours. The ic is triggered by a low-going pulse, pulling the input down to 2V/3, where V is the supply voltage. Output is normally 0V but goes high (+V) when triggered. The length of the 'on' period is:

$$t = 1.1RC$$

If the trigger pulse lasts longer than the period t, the output stays high until the trigger pulse has ended. There is no extension of the output pulse if the circuit is re-triggered. The output

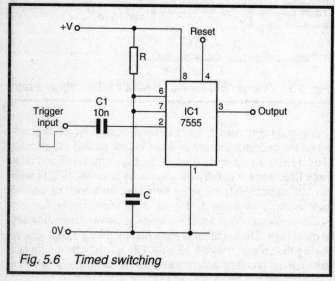

Fig. 5.6   Timed switching

142

can be reset at any time by a low-going pulse to the reset input (pin 4). If no resetting is required, the reset input pin is wired permanently to +V, but it can instead be wired to a logic output, which is normally high and is made low when the timer is to be reset. To trigger the timer with any other kind of input, do so though a 10nF capacitor.

The 7555 can source or sink up to 100mA. This makes it very easy to use as a driver and provides enough current for most applications. In Figure 5.7a the load is normally switched on because the output is at 0V. The load goes off for a period when the timer is triggered. Figure 5.7b has the opposite action which is the one more often required. The load is normally off but is switched on when the timer is triggered. Add a diode across the load if it is inductive.

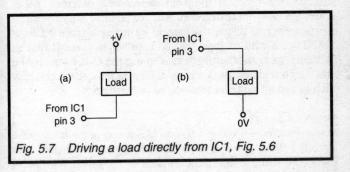

Fig. 5.7   Driving a load directly from IC1, Fig. 5.6

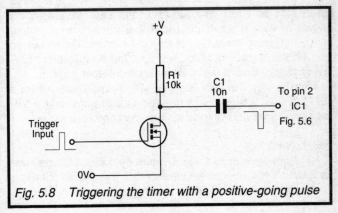

Fig. 5.8   Triggering the timer with a positive-going pulse

143

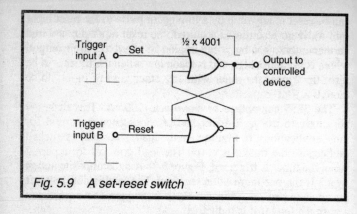

Fig. 5.9   A set-reset switch

The 7555 timer is triggered by a negative going pulse. Although most of the decoders produce positive-going pulses it is often easy to obtain the inverse by using a spare NOR or NAND gate with its inputs wired together to make it into an INVERT gate. Another method is to use the Q-bar output of a flip-flop instead of the Q output. If all else fails, the signal may be inverted by using a transistor, as in Figure 5.8.

Set-reset Switches

A set-reset flip-flop (Fig. 5.9) provides a way of switching on a device with a pulse applied to one trigger input and later switching it off with a pulse applied to the other. With NOR gates, the triggering pulse is positive-going. Negative-going pulses have no effect. The outputs of the gates are always the inverse of each other. If the flip-flop is already reset (output high), triggering the set input (input A) makes the output go low. Further triggering of the set input has no effect, but triggering the reset input (input B) makes the output go high.

The flip-flop can also be built with NAND gates (from a 4011). If so, it is triggered by negative-going inputs and the output changes are the opposite to those described above.

Toggle Switches

A J-K flip-flop with its J and K inputs both high changes state each time a pulse is received at its clock input. This allows us to switch a device on or off by sending just one pulse. The flip-

144

flop changes state at the beginning or end of the pulse. The 4027B shown in Figure 3.1 changes state on a rising edge, so it changes at the beginning of a high-going pulse or at the end of a low-going pulse. The next pulse reverses the situation. Other J-K flip-flops are available which change state on a falling edge.

The driving ability of a CMOS output is very limited so the flip-flop is generally used to drive a transistor switch.

Relays

Relays are used when there are alternating currents or large direct currents to be switched. Essentially a relay is a switch operated by an electromagnet. In some models there are several independent switches all operated by the same electromagnet but the most common kinds of switching are those illustrated in Figure 5.10. A single-pole single-throw switch may be normally open (NO) and is closed when the coil is energised. The other type of SPST switch is normally closed (NC) and is opened when the coil is energised. The changeover switch is a single-pole double-throw switch which comprises both NO and NC contacts. It switches one device on and another device off at the same instant.

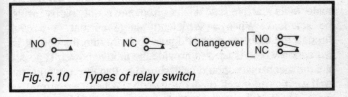

Fig. 5.10   Types of relay switch

In this book we are concerned mostly with relays that can be controlled by low-power circuits, the relay coil usually being the load of a transistor switch, as in Fig 5.3. The relay is generally rated to operate on 5V, 6V or 12V but relays will usually operate on voltages appreciably less than or greater than their nominal voltage. For example a typical relay that is nominally rated to operate at 6V may be operated on any voltage in the range 4V to 11V.

There are several types of relay, including:

Reed relays: have a high-resistance coil (500Ω or more) so they require only small currents; available in packages the same size as ics and therefore suitable for mounting on circuit-boards. Capable of switching 0.5A at up to 200V DC. Usually not suited to switching AC.

Subminiature relays: also mountable on pcbs, requiring a few tens of milliamps to operate them and capable of switching about 0.5A at mains AC voltage.

Miniature relays: Switch rather larger currents; some rated for 10A or more at mains voltage; usually about half that voltage if switching DC.

Within these groups there is a vast range of types and the reader is referred to the suppliers' catalogues. The main points to check on are the switching action, the voltage and current required to drive the relay, and the rating of the contacts.

Solenoids

A reasonable amount of motive power may be applied remotely by making use of a solenoid. Applications include operating the shutter of a camera (useful for nature photographers), opening or closing windows, operating bolts and catches. Solenoid-operated bolt and catch mechanisms can be purchased ready-made. In its inactive state the soft-iron core is only partly inside the solenoid. When a sufficiently large current is passed through the coil, the core is drawn forcibly into the coil. It is this action which is used to provide the motive power. If possible, the mechanism should be designed so that the core falls out of the coil (or is returned by a spring) when the current is switched off. This leaves it ready for a repeat action when the coil is next energised. A relatively large current is required for strong positive action. Using a coil rated for the operating voltage of the circuit, a MOSFET with low 'on' resistance is preferred. Figure 5.11 is a battery-powered circuit in which a charge is built up in high-value capacitors and then rapidly discharged through the coil by triggering the thyristor into conduction. This helps to maximise the force produced by the solenoid.

As explained above, the force produced by the solenoid draws the core into the coil. This means that the solenoid

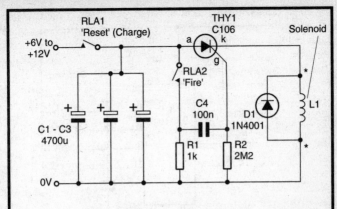

Fig. 5.11   Delivering a very high current to a solenoid. The leads to the solenoid may be extended to the points marked *.

generates a pulling force. Solenoids are also available which have a narrow rod on the core projecting through to the other end of the coil. When the coil is energised, the rod slides forcibly out of the coil, so producing a pushing force.

Stepper Motors

A stepper motor is constructed to rotate by a fixed angular amount at each step instead of rotating continuously. Most stepper motors are of the 4-phase type, which have four windings (Fig. 5.12) By energising the windings according to a prescribed sequence, the motor may be made to step either in the clockwise or the anti-clockwise direction. If it is made to rotate at high speed it appears to rotate continuously, but it can be brought to an immediate halt in any one of its 'fixed' positions. A typical stepper motor rotates $7.5°$ at each step, taking 48 steps to complete a revolution. Motors are also available that have $15°$ and $1.8°$ steps. Activation of the windings is usually placed under the control of a digital ic. The SAA1027 is a widely-used example of such an ic but there are several others available, also stepper-motor control-boards. Some of these are able to produce an extended sequence of outputs to make the motor rotate by half-steps, so producing a smoother motion.

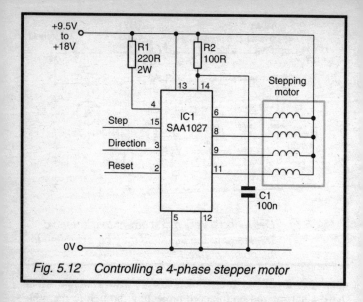

Fig. 5.12   Controlling a 4-phase stepper motor

The circuit of Figure 5.12 has 3 logic inputs. A high pulse on the STEP input makes the motor turn by one step on the rising edge of the pulse. The direction of rotation depends on the logic level at the DIRECTION input. In most motors a low input causes clockwise rotation and a high input causes anti-clockwise rotation. The RESET input is normally held high. If it is made low, the motor instantly turns to its zero position.

There are two aspects to stepper motor control. One is that by regulating the rate at which pulses are supplied, we can control the speed of rotation. Secondly, by feeding a given number of pulses to the controller ic we can control the angle through which the spindle turns - we have control of position. This latter feature is important for model and robot control.

The 7555 timer ic is useful as a pulse generator, since it works on the same voltage range as the controller ic. Figure 5.13 shows the 7555 wired to produce stepping pulses. If preferred, the output of the 7555 can be connected directly to the 'step' input of the controller. If C2 has the value 4.7μF, the pulse rate is about 0.1Hz, so the motor takes about 5s to make a complete revolution. Even slower speeds are obtainable by

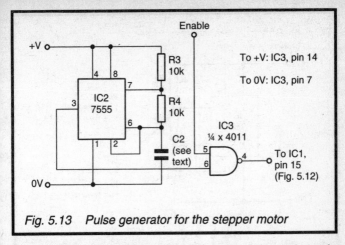

Fig. 5.13   Pulse generator for the stepper motor

increasing the value of C2 or of the resistors. Increased speeds are obtained by reducing C2; if this is 220nF, the motor rotates about 4 times per second. This is close to the maximum speed obtainable.

If the motor is to operate at a fixed speed and to be started and stopped by remote control, all that is needed is the NAND gate of Figure 5.13, acting as an enabling gate. When the enable input is high, the motor turns. This input can be controlled by a single-pulse system, or by a single digital output from any other digital system. If directional control is required too, then two latches controlled by a sequential pulse system would be the simplest solution.

The circuits outlined so far depend on a pulse generator in the controlled device, operating at a constant rate. A straightforward way of controlling the pulse rate remotely would be to arrange for resistors of different values to be switched in in place of R3, using relays. A more elegant solution to speed control is shown in Figure 5.14. IC1 generates pulses at a fixed rate, the fastest rate that is required. The pulses are fed to a counter (IC2), the outputs of which repeatedly count the binary sequence 0000 to 1111 once every sixteen pulses. The four outputs each go to an exclusive-OR gate of IC3. The other input to each gate comes from a multiple pulse decoder or from a PPM decoder. These outputs are commanded to a particular

149

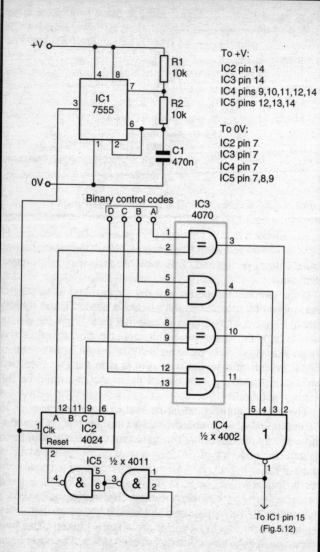

Fig. 5.14   Variable-rate pulse generator for the stepper motor

150

value between 0000 and 1111. Counting proceeds until the four output levels from IC2 are identical to those from the control latches. At this instant the outputs from all four exclusive-OR gates go low. All four inputs to the NOR gate of IC4 are low so its output goes high. A pulse is sent to the stepper motor ic and the motor steps on once. The high pulse from IC4 is also NANDed with the output from the timer. When the two inputs are high, the output of the first NAND gate goes low and that of the second NAND gate goes high. This short high pulse resets the counter to 0000. Thus IC2 counts up from 0000 until it reaches the value set by the control latches. At this point it delivers a pulse to the stepper motor and is reset back to 0000, ready to count up again. The higher the value of the input code, the longer the count takes to match that value, the less frequently the high pulse from IC4, and the more slowly the motor turns. If the input code is 0000, the counter is continually reset and the motor does not turn.

When building the circuit of Figure 5.14 it is important that the supply should be decoupled by wiring 100nF capacitors between the +V and 0V lines at several places on the circuit board. In particular, the counter ic is sensitive to supply line pulse noise, which may usually be cured by wiring a 100nF capacitor as close as possible to pins 7 and 14.

IC2 is actually a 7-stage counter so it is feasible to extend the principle of this circuit to give a finer degree of speed control.

If you are using a 418MHz radio link to control a stepper motor, remember to lay out the project so that the radio receiver module and its antenna are as far as possible from the motor or other metal parts. Usually it is best to input a 3-bit control code (step, direction, reset) into an MC145026, and to use three outputs from an MC145027 to control the three inputs to the SAA1027.

Servo Control

A servo-motor is a small high-speed motor with reduction gearing intended to rotate an arm or lever. The lever is usually able to rotate through an angle of 90°, that is to say to turn 45° on either side of a central position. Attached to the same spindle as the lever is a rotary potentiometer. The mechanism that is to be moved is attached to this lever. For example, the lever may be linked to the rudder of a boat or an elevator in an aeroplane. The potential at the wiper of the potentiometer is a measure of the angular position of the arm and hence of the part to which it is connected. The control mechanism generates a series of pulses at fixed frequency. Their length varies according to the position of a control lever. These pulses are used to flash an IR LED and the signal is picked up by an IR receiver. Alternatively, they may be sent by cable, using a line driver and receiver. The received pulses are matched against pulses generated in a special ic. The lengths of these pulses depends on the voltage generated in the rotary potentiometer in the servo-mechanism. If the signal being received does not match the signal generated in the ic, the ic switches on the motor to turn in a direction that will turn the potentiometer to make the pulse lengths equal. In this way the arm is moved to a position corresponding to that of the control lever. Because of the feedback which forms part of the matching process, this technique provides for very accurate positioning of the arm. The only proviso is that there should be a 'dead position' in which the servo switches off when the arm is close to its required position. Otherwise the servo would continuously 'hunt' on either side of the desired position. Servo-motors are widely used in radio-control of model aircraft. Constructing and setting up a servo-system requires specialist modelling or engineering skills and it is usually better, though fairly expensive, to buy the units ready-made.

A simple servo system appears in Figures 5.15 and 5.16 based on the ZN409CE servo driver ic. The transmitter incorporates a pulse generator (Fig. 5.15) which produces a series of pulses at a fixed frequency. We refer to the repetition rate of the pulses as the *frame*. In this application we set the frame to 18ms. The pulse length ranges from 1ms to 2ms. IC1 is a timer connected as an astable, with period 18ms. The exact period required is set by adjusting VR1. Once set, preferably with the aid of an oscilloscope, this period should not need to be altered. Each time the output of IC1 goes low it triggers IC2 which is connected as a monostable. The length of the pulse is set by adjusting VR2 which acts as the position control. The knob of VR2 may have a scale around it, marked with the number of degrees that the lever is to turn, or with legends such as 'hard left', 'left', 'ahead', 'right' and 'hard right'. The scale ranges

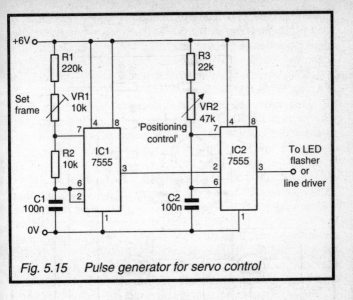

Fig. 5.15   Pulse generator for servo control

from –45° (pulse length = 1ms) through 0° (pulse length = 1.5ms) to +45° (pulse length = 2ms). The output from IC2 is used to flash IR LEDs (Fig 2.5).

An IR receiver, such as Figure 2.7, provides the input to Figure 5.16. As the servo-motor runs, the chain of reduction gears turns the arm and hence the rotary potentiometer, VR3. The voltage at the wiper, the analogue of the position of the lever is sensed by pin 3. A pulse train is generated inside the ic, with frame 18ms and pulse length ranging from 1ms to 2ms. Circuits in the ic match this against the pulse train being received at pin 14. Logic circuits switch Q1 or Q2 to drive the motor in the correct direction until the pulse trains match and the lever is in the required position. The circuit has a 'dead band' to prevent hunting.

The accuracy of a servo system depends on the track of the rotary potentiometer being strictly linear and resistant to wear. Potentiometers are available specially made for servo systems and would be found in any commercially-made servo mechanism. It you are building your own system, it is possible to use a cernet potentiometer,

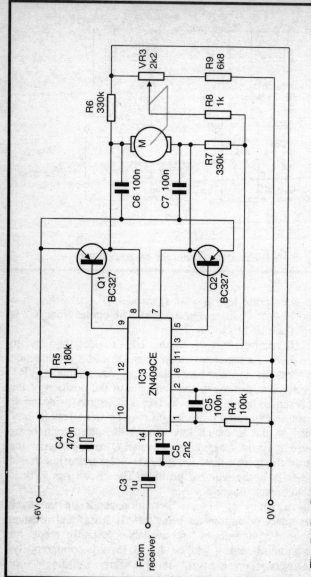

Fig. 5.16 Servo driver circuit

154

but a carbon-track potentiometer is not sufficiently reliable.

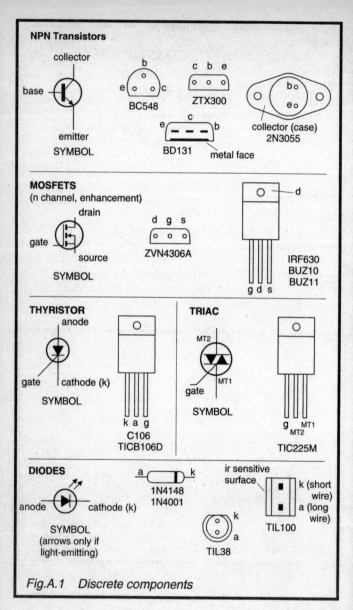

Fig.A.1   Discrete components

156

Appendix A

DATA FOR THE CONSTRUCTOR

Discrete Devices

Diagrams of terminal connections of all types mentioned in this book appear in Figure A.1. In these diagrams, the connections are shown as viewed from the underside of the device, except for the diodes which are shown in side view, and those with TO220 cases which are drawn from the 'front' (the metal tag continues down the 'back').

CMOS ICs

Diagrams of those with multiple gates appear in Figure A.2. In these diagrams, the connections are shown as viewed from above when the device is mounted on a circuit board. The terminal marked +V accepts any voltage in the range +3V to +15V. To reduce the number of drawings, the gates are represented here by standard triangular symbols.

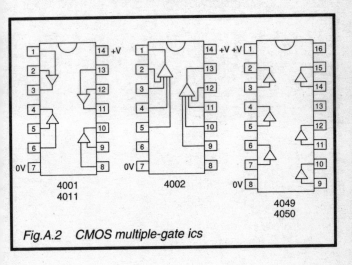

Fig.A.2   CMOS multiple-gate ics

Appendix B

USEFUL BOOKS

The following are also published by Bernard Babani (publishing) Ltd:

BP272   Interfacing PCs and Compatibles
BP273   Practical Electronic Sensors
BP316   Practical Electronic Design Data
BP377   Practical Electronic Control Projects

For a complete list of all titles, please send a stamped addressed envelope.

Appendix C

ADDRESSES OF SUPPLIERS

Maplin MPS, PO Box 777, Rayleigh, Essex SS6 8LU.
Telephone 01702 554000, Fax 01702 554001.
For most components, including radio modules.

Milford Instruments, Milford House, 120 High Street,
South Milford, Leeds LS25 5AQ.
Telephone 01977 683665. Fax 01977 681465.
BASIC Stamp.

Radio-Tech Limited, Overbridge House, Weald Hall Lane,
Thornwood Common, Epping, Essex C M16 6NB.
Telephone 0181 368 8277, International +44 1992 57 6107;
Fax 0181 361 3434, International +44 1992 56 1994.
418MHz transmitter and receiver modules, also equivalent
modules at other frequencies, for operating in other countries
worldwide.

Radiocommunications Agency, New King's Beam House, 22
Upper Ground, London SE1 9SA..
Telephone 0171 211 0502.
Copies of MPT1340. Inquiries about commercial use of the
418MHz transmitter and receiver modules, which may require
further type approval.